the Parent GAP

TOOLS TO KEEP YOUR COOL, STAY CONNECTED AND CHANGE UNHEALTHY PATTERNS

Randi Rubenstein

NEW YORK

NASHVILLE • MELBOURNE • VANCOUVER

The Parent Gap

© 2017 Randi Rubenstein

Published in New York, New York, by Morgan James Publishing in partnership with Difference Press.
www.MorganJamesPublishing.com

The Morgan James Speakers Group can bring authors to your live event. For more information or to book an event visit The Morgan James Speakers Group at www.TheMorganJamesSpeakersGroup.com.

ISBN 978-1-68350-304-0 paperback
ISBN 978-1-68350-305-7 case laminate
ISBN 978-1-68350-306-4 eBook
Library of Congress Control Number: 2016917106

Cover Design by:
John Matthew

Interior Design by:
Megan Whitney
Creative Ninja Designs
megan@creativeninjadesigns.com

Editing: Grace Kerina

Author's Photo:
Paper Heart Photography

In an effort to support local communities, raise awareness and funds, Morgan James Publishing donates a percentage of all book sales for the life of each book to Habitat for Humanity Peninsula and Greater Williamsburg.

Get involved today! Visit
www.MorganJamesBuilds.com

DEDICATION

To Scott, for being my perfect puzzle piece.

TABLE OF CONTENTS

ACKNOWLEDGMENTS

Thanks to my three kids — Alec, Avery, and Cory — for being my patient teachers... most of the time. The biggest lessons you each brought into my life are:

- Alec — the value of perspective taking and how it is the key to building a connected relationship

- Avery — triggering me as you entered the *girl world* years and helping me realize my desire to build a community of supportive sisterhood as an antidote to the destructive female social cycle

- Cory — it's not nice to talk badly behind people's backs

Thanks to my husband, Scott. We really lucked out with this life we share together—don't ya think?. You have supported and prioritized me and my work in more ways than I can even begin to list. I love you for being my detail person and looking out for me when I forget some pretty significant details. I love you for writing your own acknowledgement because I forgot to include you. Ya, I chose to write this myself but thanks. You take good care of me. I always feel loved unconditionally by you and that's something really big. Also, I think you're funny and good looking so I'm going to keep you around for a bit.

Thanks to my parents, Tommy and Barbara, for always loving me unconditionally, which gave me the self-confidence to want a better life and to seek the resources to make it happen.

Thanks to Aunt Carolyn, for being my best friend and soul sister. If you hadn't become my family through friendship, everything would have been different. I like my everything and I love you. Also, thanks for not breaking my legs as I paid back the loan.

Thanks to Peta, for your generous editing gift of lending me your "Mama" brain and perspective. The gift of time and attention towards this project truly means so much to me.

Thanks to all the friends who allowed me to pick their brains and showed up to the honest conversation vulnerably and courageously. Thank you from my whole heart.

Thanks to my Facebook community for your virtual love and support. A comment or even just a *Like* can be the pick-me-up this girl needs when I'm starring in the "going to school naked" dream.

Thanks to the mentors, teachers, and coaches who have helped me over the past eighteen years, many of whom I quoted in the book. There are too many of you to name, but it is because of your willingness to share your work that I was able to utilize you as a supportive and healing resource. This book is my tribute to your work and my contribution to pay your healing gifts forward. Your generosity in sharing your learning, teaching, and writing helped to heal me of many old wounds. I hope to follow in your footsteps.

INTRODUCTION

*"The cave you fear to enter holds
the treasure you seek."*

JOSEPH CAMPBELL

You swore to yourself that you'd do this parenting thing differently. You had big plans. Really big plans, in fact. It may have begun with an actual birth plan that involved a holistic approach to bringing life forth into the world without epidurals or C-sections. Quickly followed, of course, by skin-to-skin contact as your perfect, ten-fingered and ten-toed newborn earned breastfeeding awards for the quickest and best latch that any lactation consultant this side of the Mississippi had ever seen.

You may very well be the kind of mom who is drawn to words and phrases like *holistic* and *bringing life forth,* and there is a lot that you plan not to repeat from your own childhood. Your parents believed in McDonald's and spanking. Bathing wasn't even required daily, for the love of God. Terms like *holistic, conscious parenting,* and *mindful living* might sound like witchcraft or voodoo to

1

your parents. What you want for your kids is a far cry from the way you grew up.

The truth is, the details of that fantasy family vision are now a little hard to recall and you're pretty sure it didn't involve yelling, or tossing the little people you "brought forth" into bed as quickly as possible so that you could escape with your well-deserved first glass of wine and maybe even a cigarette. You're also fairly certain your big plan didn't include the secret desire to distract yourself with food, television, work, technology, friends, drama, substances, and almost anything other than hanging out and spending quality time with your kids. Or, perhaps, your bambinos arrived after much expense and time, through the gifts of modern science, an incredible fertility doctor, a surrogate, or adoption. (Luckily, we have many avenues available these days, especially if you have the resources to pursue your parenthood dreams.)

One thing you're pretty sure of, though, is that your fantasy didn't involve feeling so stressed out and exhausted that you were constantly in search of any way to feel better. And that the way to feel better would come in the form of standing in your pantry binge-eating your way into momentary bliss, even if it only buys you a few minutes of relief from your life.

When you begin to hear your mom's words coming out of your mouth, or you experience anger seemingly similar to your dad's temper, it is simply too freaking depressing to even admit that this is your life. You find yourself yelling day after day and it feels terrible for you and for your kids. As a result, you distract yourself to avoid thinking about your shattered plans to change this story for your kids. Facing your reality feels downright hypocritical considering that, not so long ago, you had sworn to yourself that your kids would have a better childhood than you had.

At this point, before you put this book down and head to the nearest drive-through for a French-fries-and-Frosty fix, please note that you are reading this book and this counts as a step in the right direction. Stay with me, because the information in the following pages is going to be exactly what you have needed to reconnect with your original intentions, before life happened and those dreams were temporarily put on hold.

Your dream about your fantasy family may have involved a life of hugs and memory-making moments arranged beautifully in well-organized and catalogued scrapbooks. In your fantasy, life feels more like a joyous party than that never ending Passover Seder where Aunt Hilda continues to grow drunker, louder, and less enjoyable as the hours go by at a snail's pace. Currently, your days feel unfortunately "Seder" similar.

Instead, this is the way it typically plays out when "life gets real": you have cranky, hungry people expecting you to feed them at six p.m. and your busy day didn't involve mapping out a dinner plan; you just remembered the science fair is tomorrow and your eight-year-old is panicking; soccer practice shuttling needs to happen exactly at the time that "connected families" *should* be eating dinner together; and, of course, there is a crucial work deadline hanging over your head—all while incessant whining plays as the soundtrack in the background. And on top of all that, the tension between you and your spouse is palpable.

Maybe your kids should consider themselves fortunate that all you did was raise your voice for a second or two accompanied by a few scary popping-out veiny things on your temple. I mean seriously, it could have been so much worse, right?

Unfortunately, it is the rare mom who sees her stress from a compassionate point of view and decides to give herself a hall pass when she displays her "humanness" while the shit hits the fan for a sec. In fact, these are the guilt-consumed moments we wish we could take back. These are the memories we swore would never occur on our watch. These are the moments when we secretly think to ourselves that we are repeating what was done for us and, therefore, it is determined that yes, it's true... I am screwing up my kids and they will probably end up on a therapist's couch for many years. Decades actually... talking about me and trying to recover from the terrible choices I am making right now. As. Their. Mom.

WHY ME?

When I had my oldest son, he was not an easy baby. His birth didn't go as I had planned. He was born three weeks early, the doctor used forceps, breastfeeding totally sucked for the first month, my mom stayed with us (which was way more stressful than helpful), my baby cried so much more than he slept, and—on top of all that—motherhood happened three years before I was planning on it. Needless to say, it was a dark time when it was *supposed* to be only beautiful and special. Basically, the guilt began at the very beginning for me.

My motherhood journey over the last 18 years has been an interesting ride. I've experienced healing from old wounds and knocks on my front door from unfinished business that I had no idea was secretly still stalking me. I believe I have been able to completely change the trajectory for myself and my family, and the results of that journey can feel like a high. This is especially appealing to me, someone who was numb to the sensations in my body and has struggled with an addiction-prone mind and behavior patterns since I was a teenager.

I believe the concepts represented in these pages have assisted me in changing some pretty dysfunctional patterns within my family tree, resulting in the healing of past, present, and future generations. To me, these strategies have the potential to be as transformative, powerful, and healing in your life as they have been in mine. It is my absolute pleasure to share them with you.

I have spent many years researching, studying, applying, and teaching these concepts in my own life. As a connector, I have a deep desire to share the wealth. My philosophy is that the flavor of that decadent piece of chocolate cake intensifies and becomes way more delicious if I hand out forks to other chocoholics and we get to enjoy each bite together and discuss the deliciousness. This coaching work and my passion for supporting parents in building connected families is my way of giving you a fork and inviting you to dig in and savor the flavor.

The secret worry: *screwing up your biggest assignment in life—raising your kids* resonates with many parents. I don't think many of us speak about this out loud and we may not even be aware of it on a conscious level. I know I wasn't.

A few years ago, I sent out a survey to pick the brains of mom's in my community. A woman that I didn't know all that well at the time, answered my questionnaire in a way that caused me to have that goose-bump sensation—you know the one, right?

When I asked about her biggest concern, she answered, "I'm just so worried I might be f#*king up my kids and they will spend the rest of their lives in therapy." Once that "Aha!" came my way, I realized that raising my kids and sending them into adulthood as emotionally and physically healthy as possible was the driving force behind my mission as a mom all along. And now that *honest-answering-questionnaire* mom happens to be one of my best friends and soul sisters. How could she not be? Her "real-ness" and "f-bombs" spoke to my soul. She became my first client, and I am continuously blown away by the changes she has solidified in her life and family. As I think about her and how she has added to my life, it feels like evidence that there are no coincidences. It was always intended for me to "sit next to her" in this lifetime.

THE PARENTING EVOLUTION

I have come to believe that the human cycle of development and the way we are meant to evolve reflects in each generation knowing a little more and improving the systems handed down to us from the one preceding. According to this model, I tell my kids, "Hopefully y'all will be even better parents when it's your turn." This is evolution. This is how it is meant to be.

How has *The Parenting Evolution* affected my life? I think it will be illuminating to explain a little of the backstory about my folks. My parents are kind and loving people who are very much a part of my life today. They love my kids like crazy and are very involved in our lives. If you need a ride to the airport, someone to keep your dogs when you go on vacation, or help of any kind, my dad is your guy. My mom would love to make you a tuna fish sandwich, so feel free to drop by her house anytime. They would do anything under the sun for my family. Just to be clear, this is not a book trashing them. Like many of you, I grew up in the 1970s and 1980s. It was a different time. The truth is, my parents—and probably yours too—did the best they could with the information they had at the time.

I have never been a "woe is me" type of person. My protective armor was one of "having it together" and even deflecting from my problems to help you with yours. Can you relate? I know that many of you have stood alongside me in the "tough-chick sorority." Admitting there is weakness, humanness, and vulnerability felt foreign and uncomfortable to me. So, at 27, when I had a baby that never seemed to stop crying, I pretended I had a plan and knew what I was doing. Secretly, I was fact-finding my little heart out, searching for solutions about what to freaking do to actually figure this motherhood thing out and how to put this crying baby down so I could make a sandwich. And just so you know, the original front loading baby carrier, the Baby Bjorn, literally saved me from starvation by freeing up my sandwich making hands while holding my fussy boy.

Speaking of my appetite, I had an insatiable hunger for information about babies and parenting and pretty much anything I could get my hands on that landed in those two categories. And, just so you know, that was extremely out of character for my tough-chick, cigarette-loving self. My husband, Scott, often commented that I read and studied during that time like a college stu-dent the night before a semester final.

I now know—because of my results from taking my favor-ite personal assessment test, Kolbe A Index (https://secure.kolbe.com/k2/show_takeIndex/indexType_A) – that my brain takes action when given a challenging task by researching like a madwoman, jumping in, and trying new skills as I learn them. My quest for knowledge when facing beginning motherhood challenges makes perfect sense to me. (I will tell you more about the Kolbe test later in the book.)

As a person who guarded myself with a tough outer shell, I never went to therapy or read any self-help books before I became a mom. When I was growing up, my family would have probably described those things as dramatic and even flaky. Yet when I became a mom and began reading parenting books and experimenting with new strategies in my test kitchen with my kiddos, I felt empowered by what I was learning.

Through a series of events and, basically, a backdoor approach, I began teaching parenting classes to other moms and dads. My workshops were based on a discipline model that is typically used by teachers to manage their students through encouragement and positive strategies called Conscious Discipline (https://consciousdiscipline.com). I translated the program from the classroom to the home and turned it into a conscious parenting program. I loved sharing personal stories of struggle and success with other parents about what was working in our family as we used Conscious Discipline strategies as our underlying guide.

Back then, conscious parenting was not a common buzz phrase. If you are unfamiliar with the term *conscious parenting*, you can easily find out more nowadays—the great Oprah-endorsed guru, Dr. Shefali Tsabary, is a wealth of knowledge on this topic. Dr. Shefali describes conscious parenting as an approach where children serve as mirrors of their parents' forgotten selves. She teaches about a parent's willingness to look into the metaphorical mirror that your children hold before you and the opportunity it will create to establish a relationship with your own inner state of wholeness. This rather *heady* explanation summed up my experience as a mom over the years. Motherhood had been my most spiritual experience to date. Okay fine. You got me. It was the ONLY real spiritual experience that I could identify. As a *cultural* Jewish girl, meaning I never considered myself religious, I wasn't even sure what spirituality meant and frankly, that sort of thing sounded like the opposite of my *cup of coffee.* Tea was not my thing either. My inner reflection could be seen in my kids, and my desire not to pass down my childhood wounds to them put just the right amount of fire under my tush to face my unfinished business and heal. And I have done most of this healing through self-study and by building connected relationships with my husband and kids. It hasn't involved loads of money in therapy costs or doctor visits. In the past few years, I have invested in coaching programs and they have helped me tremendously. We live in an information-rich time and there are tons of healing tools easily accessible from the comfort of your bed... my favorite classroom and where I write these words to you right now.

For me, conscious parenting is about retraining your brain to be present or fully conscious in the current moment with your kids so that you can think clearly when life gets challenging...as it often does with our own kids. I describe being a conscious parent as retraining your brain because as I will describe in more detail throughout these pages, most humans operate from old subconscious programming rather than the conscious part of your brain you fill with the new information you might be learning right now as you read this.

When life gets hard and your stress hormones kick in, you may find yourself yelling, threatening or ignoring, even though that is totally out of alignment with the supportive and loving parent you want to be. The parent you are in your heart. The old programs deep within your brain that you may have experienced as a kid when you were admonished by your parents, coaches, and teachers, which contain the words and reactions you swore you would never use, come flooding back when your buttons are pushed. Many parents think the answer to this is to control your kids and force them to stop pushing your buttons. Unfortunately, as most of us have experienced, that doesn't work and usually makes the situation worse and your children more defiant because most people rally and rebel when others attempt to power over and aggressively control you. Our kids are no different.

Becoming a conscious parent involves a willingness to face hard issues that are still with you from your own childhood, and the courage to work at creating new patterns rather than repeating ones that didn't feel good for you as a kid. I believe that if you are reading this right now, you have received the conscious call to action to become part of *The Parenting Evolution*. This is what I call the movement of conscious parents that are ready to replace destructive familial patterns with healthier ones. There IS a better way to growing kids than the way many of us were raised and it doesn't involve violent words or behaviors. This new style of parenting is focused on having productive conversations with your kids and becoming a connected family team. It will feel good for you and your kids will thrive under this model. I believe this style of conscious parenting will change the world by raising the next generation with more nourishing methods and the outcome will be healthy, kind and fulfilled people.

I now know that teaching parenting classes served a huge purpose on my path. It kept me honest and accountable with my kids because if I was going to show up each week to teach parenting, I had to really believe that it worked. By weaving the Conscious Discipline curriculum into my personal family stories, I was able to teach parenting concepts and methods in an engaging and relatable way.

Teaching through story is a powerful and effective way to learn, but as I constantly worked to combine my real life examples with dry and typically boring parenting concepts, *pedestal syndrome* kept creeping in. *Pedestal syndrome* has to do with placing someone who's in an authoritative role on a pedestal and feeling like they are special and not the norm. I often heard other parents say, hopelessly, "I just wish I could think of the exact right thing to say, like you do, when I'm in the moment with my kids." What these parents were actually referring to was my ability to stay calm and think clearly when my kids were being difficult. I didn't realize this at the time but I do now. I'm now able to share my recipe and more effectively help frustrated parents hold themselves accountable and solidify healthier patterns. My goal is to fully support other parents, that have taken the time and energy to learn a new conscious way of parenting, to be successfully calm and clear headed during hard moments with your kids.

The theme to closing *The Parent Gap* is: *Calm people solve problems.* When you are able to remain calm, you can think clearly and manage yourself in a way that never induces guilt later. As you master and model this incredibly beneficial skill for your kids, they become calm problem-solving people as well. Isn't that the point of learning parenting tools and reeducating yourself? It's not like you're wracking your brain for a different way to handle your kids when they are easy and cooperative. It's during the heated times when your kids are ignoring you; you're running late and they have no sense of urgency; your toddler has a meltdown in the middle of Target over a toy or piece of candy you told him to put back; your preteen gives you lip and speaks disrespectfully while your parents look on like they are spectators at the US Open...it's during those times when your buttons are pushed and your blood is boiling that you need access to the conscious parenting tools that I speak about.

As a conscious parent, you will learn how to remain calm so that you can handle your button-pushing child in a way that successfully teaches her the way you expect her to behave without making you the enemy in her eyes. Conscious parenting is NOT permissive parenting.

Conscious parents are the calm, assertive, clear-headed CEOs of the family. This is not a case of *the clowns running the circus*—your kids will be crystal clear that you are the *ringmaster.*

As parents, many of us experience a frustrating *gap* between the parent you always planned to be; the calm connected parent your kiddos crave AND the parent you currently are during challenging moments with your kids...the version of yourself that yells and behaves in ways you swore you never would. This gap causes a lot of guilt and remorse for us parents and many of us are embarrassed to admit this reality to ourselves—let alone others. I call this gap, *The Parent Gap,* and this book addresses how to close the gap by keeping your cool during heated moments with the people you love most in the world.

"When you know better, you do better."

MAYA ANGELOU

THE PARENT GAP

Pedestal syndrome and the "I'm a hopeless parent" script I kept hearing, sent me on yet another quest for knowledge. Only this time, I kept saying, "I need tools." I knew I needed something else, but I couldn't put my finger on what that something was yet. The reality, as I saw it, was that many families were living in a state of "functional misery," and I wanted to be a part of the solution in changing that and in supporting parents in their search for happier paths for their families. My hunch told me that they needed more than conscious parenting classes to help them escape the unhappiness and create their connected dream family.

I set out on a quest for knowledge. I considered various counseling and coaching avenues and finally settled on an author, and one of the original life coaches, Martha Beck (http://marthabeck.com/) She is Harvard-educated, super smart, kinda quirky, and one of Oprah's people. The perfect combo of traits for me. I am a sucker for an Oprah endorsement, even though that might make me seem kinda mainstream and unoriginal. But it's the truth. I've been a super-fan since *The Color Purple*. I had a feeling that Martha's coaching tools were just the things to help me figure out the quandary between learning conscious parenting strategies and actually being able to apply them in real life. Again, I refer to this gap as *The Parent Gap*. It's the gap between *what you want to do as a parent and what you actually do during a triggered moment with your kids*. My mission is to help you close *The Parent Gap*; managing your kids in a calm controlled way, even during the times when you want to strangle them. Ultimately, creating the family you've always desired.

Time and time again, I've heard from parents: "Why do I constantly feel like I'm doing it wrong? I'm not 'supposed' to yell at my kids or ignore them or, even worse, be annoyed by them. I feel so guilty. All. The. Time."

If you have ever thought, "What if my children tell me, years from now, that they're in therapy because of what I did?" I'm writing this book for you. This book is for all parents: those who have never heard the term *conscious parenting* and those who have learned parenting strategies over the years but have felt unsuccessful in applying them. This book addresses *The Parent Gap* because, in my opinion, it's a big ol' waste of time to learn stuff that sounds great in theory but never translates in reality.

Parenting tools simply don't work without mastery of the foundational concepts I will teach you over our time together. I'm so glad you're here. These tools are the real deal. I'm not a professional on a pedestal theorizing about what "should" work. I'm a parenting coach. Even more importantly, I'm a fellow mom on the ground, just like you, living every day with my family, and raising my kids with these foundational tools. Without the information I will teach you, I would have had a much less happy life.

THE MAMA WARRIOR COMMUNITY

In the stories I tell throughout these pages, the client names have been changed. Duh. I'm like the Mafia with my people. I never saw you. I never heard anything. Capisce?

I hope you feel my warm, supportive mama-to-mama hug throughout these pages. I want you to stop feeling alone and know there is a community waiting for you, if you accept our invitation. I am going to bring up a lot of things we don't typically discuss as moms—secrets not to be discussed in daylight, the stuff many of us do to cope and feel better and then end up feeling guilty about, the things we often choose to do instead of being actively engaged with our kids. I refer to these things as *distractions*. We all have them. I have them even today. The goal is not to live a 100 percent distraction-free life. The goal is about balance, and learning what works for you and your family. And another thing—you don't need to feel pressured to quit doing that thing that enables you to feel better right now. You are the boss of your life, and you will know when it's time to lessen or send that distraction packing. I'm not here to judge you for doing what you need to do to feel better and make it through the day right now.

I do have an antidote that will help you end the painful cycle, as well as strategies you can learn that will help you to do so. You can feel surrounded by a loving community and have the understanding that you are not alone on Bad Mama Island anymore. Ultimately, the process you will be taken through will give you real, actionable steps to help rescue you from your current pattern, which will allow you to create the connected family you crave and, of course, to feel better. Because in feeling better, you will feel less of a need to *cope* by using that "thing" that allows you to numb, escape, or distract yourself into feeling momentarily good.

As your life begins to resemble the way it looked when you fantasized about your future family, years ago, the whole world will begin to look different. I'm so excited to hand you that gift, wrapped up as this book, knowing how much you are going to love the relief that's on its way.

WOULD YOU LIKE A BITE OF CAKE?

It has been brought to my attention recently that maybe only a few of us—me, my friend Christine, and about five of you who are reading this book—actually read parenting books cover to cover. Apparently, most of us buy them, read the first chapter, and don't get much further (hopefully you're still reading now). As a "chocolate cake sharer," I'm all too happy to provide the Cliff Notes of my journey, represented in this book. For some reason, parenting and self-help books are like riveting novels for me. I have always had a sense that time is of the essence when it comes to raising kids. Since becoming a mom, I've had a type of maternal, magnetic pull that lit a fire within me to learn, test, and implement strategies about how to raise kids to be as emotionally healthy as possible. Being a person who didn't always feel all that emotionally healthy, I was literally cramming and racing against the clock as a parent. I knew I had a lot to learn, and my kids were rapidly developing each month. Today, after years of experimentation with the tools and strategies I was implementing in my "test kitchen," I am ready to share these methods with you.

I will explain in the following chapters why *The Parent Gap* occurs and the remedy. What I have learned is that all of the best parenting tools will not improve your life and family if there is an inability to access the file in your brain with the information at crunch time. It is important to understand this process so that you can learn how to retrain your brain to access the correct file when you really need it.

TOOLS TO KEEP YOUR COOL AND THINK CLEARLY TO CLOSE THE PARENT GAP

The framework you will be taken through in this book includes:

- identifying the unhealthy patterns in your life so you know where to begin;

- understanding your need to cope with your current circumstances and why distractions have been necessary;

- learning to hear the whispers of your body;

- having the courage to learn your story and really look at it through the lens of a curious observer;

- acting as a family history archaeologist, excavating stories and patterns passed down from past generations;

- stepping into the role of being your own super-fan and learning to celebrate and cheer for yourself;

- letting go of perfection to embrace the ultimate goal of *connection*; and

- learning to lock your door and ban the guilt monster from entering your sacred home.

If you're an instant gratification seeker like me, you're going to love this fast-action formula. I created it as a way to give you the jump-start and support you most likely haven't had, so you can realign with the intention in your heart to be the proud Mama Warrior, creating the connected family you fantasized about years ago.

CHAPTER 1

CHANGING UNHEALTHY PATTERNS

"When you hold on to your history, you do it at the expense of your destiny."

BISHOP TD JAKES

SO THIS HAPPENED...

Gigi was referred to me by a tutor who was working with her daughter. Gigi was concerned that her eighth-grade, high-achieving daughter was beginning to slide academically, and nothing Gigi said or suggested was being taken seriously. The upset mother felt like her hands were tied as she watched her daughter's former academic success slowly being dragged down in a pit of quicksand. Gigi described her daughter as avoiding contact and basically shutting her out.

The air felt heavy and thick with tension between Gigi and her daughter, where they had been very close in the past. Their communication was limited to Gigi's questions that resulted in brief and seemingly annoyed responses from her teenage daughter. That scenario is all too common between mothers and their teen daughters, so Gigi wasn't sure if she should take the behavior personally or just chalk it up to typical adolescent girl behavior.

Gigi sought my support for help with strategies so she could help her daughter get back on the success track to "reach her potential." High school was around the bend and the clock was ticking toward when the grades would begin to "truly matter."

I began by asking Gigi questions about her own teenage years. She hadn't thought about those memories in years and, at first, had a hard time recalling the information. But once she started remembering, she was able to tell me many stories about her own teen years. I heard the disdain in her voice pretty much immediately toward her own mom. I had a feeling that Gigi's teenage experience—and specifically the role and effect of her mother—would be a pivotal piece to her daughter's plummeting-grades puzzle.

Initially, Gigi described her worry to be all about her daughter's academic performance and future success. She honestly believed there was nothing more to figure out, but—as I'm sure you probably realize—there was.

Gigi would say now that underneath that worry about her daughter's achievement-oriented future was the real concern. Gigi felt the tension and shutdown and secretly worried that she was royally screwing up her daughter. She was pained by the thought that her little girl, who she loved more than life itself, would continue to shut her out—just as Gigi had done with her own mother. Gigi didn't realize that her big fear was actually all about the repetition of the unhealthy pattern she had experienced with her own mother.

It turned out that Gigi's daughter's troublesome school performance was connected to the childhood patterns Gigi had been subconsciously continuing with her own daughter. They were the same themes or patterns she'd had as a girl with her own mother, and which caused her years of anger and resentment. It's no wonder that, during our initial meeting, Gigi mentioned that she hadn't recalled memories from her teen years in a very long time. Those years represented a time she was all too happy to leave where it belonged—in the past.

Once Gigi began to uncover some of the unwelcome and uninvited patterns from her own childhood, she was able to see how the same patterns were showing up in her relationship with her daughter. Of course, those patterns were cleverly disguised and, even though Gigi's intent came from a place of love and putting her daughter's future success at the forefront, the same patterns were nonetheless being repeated. When Gigi was able to see this cleverly disguised pattern clearly, she ripped off that lame mustache. You know the one—the cockeyed *stache* with the missing adhesive that Rooster wore as he and Bernadette Peters' character tried to steal Annie from Daddy Warbucks? When Gigi was able to do the "Rooster Reveal" on those old, unwelcome patterns, she was able to make some amazing shifts.

Being the quick study and the extremely loving mother that she was, Gigi turned the relationship around in no time. Currently, the mama-daughter duo is enjoying a beautiful relationship consisting of fly-fishing expeditions, bedside television binge-watch-a-thons, and constant dialogue about the demands of high school.

As Gigi discovers triggers from her own teen years that resurface as her daughter is in the thick of it, instead of repeating the pattern between her mother and herself, she's taking steps to end the unhealthy cycle. She is supporting her daughter as she would love to have been supported by her own mother when she was a girl.

This is the beauty of uncovering and changing unhealthy patterns.

CONSCIOUS PARENTING LESSON AND SKILL: YOUR *WHY*

Why do you want to raise your kids differently? Knowing your reason can make all the difference.

Uncovering your *why* will shed light on the patterns you want to change and why they didn't feel good for you growing up.

Write a few lines in your journal about why it's important to you to raise your kids differently than how your parents raised you. This exercise will be hugely beneficial as you continue reading, thinking, learning, and reflecting throughout this book.

When you write in your journal, it's important to tap into your right brain and access the information of your heart rather than writing from your left brain. Your left brain involves your ego and may keep you from even beginning to journal, because the ego wants to sound really impressive and smart. Your left brain will imagine someone else reading your journals and this will be a roadblock in uncovering your *why*.

To access your right brain—your intuitive inner knowing —write in a stream of consciousness manner. This is also called a *brain dump*—you dump every thought on paper, without using grammar or punctuation. It may look like the journal of a crazy person. For example: "im writing to write because im upset what am i upset about i just dont feel happy because we arent on the same page but now i dont know what to write and i will keep writing until i think of something oh ya now i remember i want to lose weight and i feel obsessed about that and i want to be a better mom..."

If you are not the journaling type, I get it. First of all, drop the vision of that beautiful Oprah-esque bedside table journal and adopt the realistic version of journaling just for yourself. For me, this usually involves typing into the Notes section on my iPhone while I'm in the carpool line. The point is to get the thoughts that are trapped in your brain *out,* so you can process and uncover your *why*. Practicing this skill through the written or typed word brings tremendous clarity that you simply won't experience by only thinking about it.

CONSCIOUS PARENTING TOOL: PRESENT ENGAGED TIME (P.E.T.)

Even if you aren't buying in yet and have no idea how to parent "consciously" to change your patterns, it is important to do just one thing each day that represents your future self. You know, the "you" who never yells at her kids and who actually enjoys dressing Barbie. It doesn't really matter what the activity itself is. Spend five to fifteen minutes engaged with your kids where they get to decide the activity and you give them 100% of your undivided attention. I call this a P.E.T. (Present Engaged Time). Preferably this is a one-on-one activity, so if you have multiple kiddos, do this with each kid. *Stop freaking out.* Five minutes is the amount of time it takes for my middle-aged bladder to fully empty. You've got this. Of course, you can do this for more than five minutes if you want to, but five minutes is a doable amount of time to begin with.

One hundred percent engaged presence between the two of you will fill your child's attention-seeking love cup immensely. It is an extremely effective way to pad your relationship bank account and ward off meltdowns that frequently occur because your child is actually looking for a way to connect with you. Young children often act out in ways that seek negative attention when they aren't receiving enough engagement with you. All attention counts for young kids. It really doesn't matter all that much to little kids if the attention is negative or positive.

Being an engaged and present parent by practicing the P.E.T. tool for even a few minutes a day will begin changing the patterns within your family and create more connection between you and your child. Becoming a conscious parent by proactively engaging in daily P.E.T.s with your child will pay off for everyone in the family in the long run.

This tool works on many levels, and will help your child feel loved, seen, enjoyed, and, as a result, she will be more cooperative afterward. This will make your child more enjoyable to be around, and more opportunities will present themselves for you and her to hang out together and have fun. This will build connection and relieve guilt for you. This tool is a great starting point, and the benefits will happen immediately.

I am super excited for you to experience how little time this takes and how much bang for your buck you will get from it in terms of cooperation from your child.

* * *

Now that you know the first foundational concept (identifying and changing unhealthy patterns) for closing *The Parent Gap,* you can begin to notice familiar nuances from your own upbringing. To be able to give your kids a different experience from your own, it is important to recognize the patterns you want to change in order to know where to begin.

Even though my coaching philosophy is definitely present- and future-focused, the past does have to be addressed when it comes to creating new patterns. It is so much easier to identify what you don't want and build a model of your dream family from that place, rather than starting at square one with a blank sheet of paper. Our fantasies regarding motherhood usually involve improving upon the way we were raised. We don't have to bad-mouth our parents and feel disloyal and guilty in order to improve the patterns.

Remember that this is about *The Parenting Evolution* —each generation has access to more information and, hopefully, to doing things a little better than the generation before. So let's do what actually works, not just what sounds good. That might sound a bit negative, but it's effective. You are playing with high stakes here, and you take this seriously. This is about your kids, after all, and the family you may have been fantasizing about since you were in the fifth grade. Or is that just me?

CHAPTER 2

DISTRACTIONS ARE COPING STRATEGIES

"What you resist, persists."

C. G. JUNG

SO THIS HAPPENED...

Shelley, a mild-mannered 34-year-old mother of three beautiful kids ages six, four, and two, loves her job and family. She and her husband have been together since their late teens. Her parents live a mere neighborhood away and are very involved in the young family's life and in the raising of their three precious kids. Shelley has a few groups of friends and there is always a text or phone call to return regarding a pending social invitation. Her life *appears* to be blessed. Full.

Shelley tells me that she actually feels all alone most of the time. Her weight yo-yos up and down and mostly the scale maintains at a number that's 30-50 pounds higher than her ideal weight. She beats herself up about her lack of discipline and her irresponsibility regarding exercise, and she struggles because she feels unworthy of a hug. In her words, "I am repulsive."

Shelley wants the world for her kids and feels she is doing everything she can for them. However, the air in their home is thick with tension. She and her husband have no physical relationship; her oldest child struggles with intense anxiety; the temper tantrums are plentiful; and the laughter is sparse. Although her parents are a constant presence in their lives and *live for the kids,* Shelley feels judged and demeaned by them—especially by her mother.

Shelley's mother has always been a *yeller* and even though Shelley swore she would NEVER follow in her mother's footsteps, she frequently hears her mother's words and tone coming out of her own mouth—especially with her oldest child during his anxious meltdowns. Shelley knows her reactions are not helpful. As she experienced as a girl herself, a mother's harsh words can be quite emotionally harmful to her anxious child. Throughout Shelley's life, she has been afflicted with anxiety as well and feels tremendously guilty for her behavior towards her son during these moments. And still the vicious cycle continues.

It is incredibly triggering for Shelley when her son refuses to go somewhere or have a new experience because he is held back by an anxiety-induced panic attack. Quite often, Shelley, contributes to his anxiety by raising her voice and using harsh shaming language. What her sweet boy really needs is for his mom to be his *soft place to land* during these intense moments. It is painful for Shelley to witness her son's anxious behavior or to reflect back on her own after these challenging times. Shelley remedies her guilt hangover later with sugary processed foods usually in the form of cookies and donuts. This is her drug of choice to cope with the repeating destructive pattern of anxiety, yelling and disconnection that has most likely been a part of her family tree for generations.

The interesting thing is that Shelley's wide variety of Facebook posts involving pics of her beautiful kiddos in their coordinating outfits and posed smiles suggest she is *livin' the dream*. In private, her kid's frequent tantrums drive her crazy and although she loves them with all her heart, she rarely enjoys their company. Deep down, she worries that she is a bad mom. Shelley wants to be the mom she dreamed of when she was a girl, but she finds herself constantly distracted by her phone, work, and social media notifications commenting on her cutie pie pics she posted of the kids, rather than actually engaging with them.

The guilt sets in because Shelley wants to be different, and knows she *should* be more present and attentive, but for some reason she can't explain, she continues the same pattern. Her guilt and underlying shame are just too much. So she continues to distract herself with anything and everything to avoid the discomfort of her reality. This cycle continues day after day, year after year. As the saying goes, "The days are long but the years are short." She feels a long way off from getting this sorted out, and she is worried that time is running out to turn things around. The thought that swirls in her mind when her head hits the pillow and all she wants is for her exhausted body to finally rest is, "What if my kids end up being screwed up and blame me?" At two a.m. she finally gets up and heads to the kitchen for a "late-night fog" eating binge on whatever she can find to try and feel better and make the negative thinking stop so she can finally fall asleep.

We are living in an era of female loneliness. Author Tommy Rosen (http://www.tommyrosen.com/yoga) calls it "the adult female epidemic... the need to numb." He says that "love leads to security, strength, and health. Trauma leads to disease within your body, which leads to looking away aided by some kind of addictive behavior." It turns out that Shelley's trauma is that she has never truly felt loved. Her mother has an explosive temper and has been highly critical of Shelley's body for as far back as she can remember. Her mom called her "a moose" and other horrible names when Shelley was a child. Shelley has always believed that she is a disappointment, based on the size of her body and her anxious personality. She feels tremendous shame about her weight and her lack of control regarding diet and exercise. After explosive episodes with her own anxious child, she feels like a failure on multiple levels.

What Shelley doesn't yet understand is that food has been her savior throughout the years. She has used food as her drug to help her cope and to feel better, due to the scars caused by a lifetime of emotional abuse—abuse that cut her self-esteem to shreds because the bully in her life was her own mother.

We all know that food is fuel. We need it to survive. What many don't understand, especially those of us who struggle with emotional eating, is that food can also be used as a drug. It literally alters you biochemically. Certain foods—specifically, processed foods laden with sugar, additives, salt, and saturated fat—temporarily provide the same effects as Prozac. The food numbs the emotional pain by releasing a dopamine hit. That's what happens for Shelley.

When Shelley is lying in bed unable to fall asleep and feeling like a terrible mom, stuck in her shame cycle of *yelling-eat-repeat*, the pain is just too great, so she gets up and, in an almost robotic trance, seeks out her drug of choice: carbs and sugar—the substance that she has sub-consciously learned will give her a dopamine hit and allow her to feel better. She doesn't think about it. She doesn't think of the illogical reasoning and the logical consequence... a body that is 40 pounds heavier than she desires.

This cycle is all too common. We are humans living a human experience. All any of us want is to feel good. To feel good in our bodies, minds, and lives. We often live on autopilot, seeking that feeling of *good*, or at least *better than*, our current state. The fact is that one out of four adult American women take antidepressants. One out of four! Experts say this behavior of seeking biochemical altering is bordering on an epidemic. Women feel alone, crave a real sense of belonging, and are searching for superficial ways to feel better in this human experience.

I call the need to numb, escape, and distract a *coping strategy*. Binge eating to increase dopamine levels in order to feel better has been Shelley's coping strategy. Without it, who knows what she would have done? The question is, how much longer can Shelley sustain this bleak existence? Talk about not thriving—she is hanging on by a very thin thread.

Luckily, Shelley's son's extreme symptoms of panic and anxiety, propelled the tortured mom to reach out for help. Shelley is learning about herself and her own story. She is building tremendous strength and courage daily to discover new techniques for feeling better, rather than binge eating. She is learning new parenting tools and retraining her subconscious brain to be able to handle her anxious child's behaviors the way she would have loved herself when she was growing up. She hasn't yelled in months and not coincidentally, her son's anxiety has decreased considerably. Shelley is beginning to set boundaries with her parents and is becoming more assertive as a daughter, wife, mother, friend and woman in general. Shelley is changing destructive family patterns, and she has begun to lay her head down at night feeling a little more peaceful than she felt the day before. The laughter she envisioned years ago as she daydreamed about her fantasy family has entered the home. As her home life continues to improve she is also pleased to report her shrinking body size. Although she hasn't reached her size 4 "goal", she is not far off and has lost thirty pounds. Right now, that feels pretty great.

CONSCIOUS PARENTING LESSON AND SKILL: UNDERSTANDING AND IDENTIFYING DISTRACTION PATTERNS

Why do we have a need to distract ourselves and how does it affect our parenting? Understanding the scientific explanation behind our desire to feel better is an important piece of the puzzle.

As humans, our brains are full of chemicals, including neurotransmitters. Neurotransmitters are the chemicals responsible for transmitting signals in between neurons in the brain. Dopamine is the neurotransmitter in charge of our pleasure-reward system. It allows us to feel enjoyment and bliss. Having too little dopamine can leave us unfocused, unmotivated, lethargic, and possibly depressed. It is thought that people low in dopamine lack a zest for life. When this occurs, we look for external ways to increase our dopamine levels. I refer to these activities as distractions. Some distractions, or coping mechanisms, that increase dopamine levels take the form of types of food or activities, such as caffeine, sugar, junk food, stimulants, drugs, drinking, technology, smoking, shopping, gossiping, binge watching, working, excessive exercise, etc. Every time you look at the screen of your smartphone, your brain receives a little dopamine hit. This is why many of us are literally addicted to our devices.

Many of us and our children have sizable sugar addictions. This is the real gateway drug, in my opinion. Sugar and alcohol dependencies have freakishly similar effects on the body. Many baby formulas even have added sugar. Chicago pediatric dentist Dr. Kevin Boyd, who has a master's degree in nutrition and dietetics, teaches that, "We're conditioning them to crave sweetness. I would say any formula that has sucrose... causes sugar cravings. It triggers the release of dopamine in the brain, and it's a comfort-level thing."

It seems possible that since we were babies many of us have been addicted to and reliant on sugar to feel balanced biochemically. This could be a possible factor contributing to our use of distracting behaviors to feel better and to increase our dopamine levels. It is very difficult to be in the present moment with your kids when you are stuck on the external dopamine search committee.

As an addiction-prone person myself, I can attest to the fact that anytime I need a substance to feel better, it is extremely hard for me to be present in the moment. If you get truly honest with yourself, how many times are you with your kids but thinking about that "thing" that will make you feel better? It is a vicious cycle, because the more you escape the present moment to feel better, the guiltier and worse you probably feel later when alone with your thoughts. This ends up contributing to even more distraction to relieve the guilt to feel better, and on and on and on. This is the cycle of shame-distraction-guilt, in no particular order.

WHY ARE OUR DOPAMINE LEVELS LOW IN THE FIRST PLACE?

As humans, we have a basic need for love and belonging. This is achieved through connecting relationships, through family and community. When this need is not being met, our dopamine levels are low, which causes us not to feel good. To cope with these less-than-awesome feelings, we seek ways to increase our dopamine levels and feel better—resulting in our reliance on distractions. This is why I refer to distractions as *coping strategies*. You have been subconsciously looking for ways to feel better and, therefore, the food, technology, drugs, or whatever the distraction you typically choose has been an effective way to temporarily feel better but it has become a habitual pattern.

Many of us have no idea that we are stuck in this cycle. Like Shelley, we may be surrounded with friends, family, social commitments, and what looks like a very full life. However, how often do we simply go through the motions in our lives? How often do you leave a situation feeling depleted rather than energized? Who do you engage with in your life such that you never second-guess what you've said or worry that they will spill your secrets? Shelley's life appears to be fulfilling her need for love and belonging—she has three kids, involved parents, a husband, clients, and loads of friends—yet she feels completely alone and "closet-eats" for comfort. I'm afraid this is more common than not.

The female loneliness epidemic afflicts many moms. This is not something that's openly discussed and, frankly, it's a bit of a taboo subject. As I see it, there is an underlying female competitive vibe in our culture and this leaves our belonging needs unmet. We strive to not only be great parents, but to show others that we're great parents. Think about the mommy wars, re: working/not working, school choices, school involvement, children's academic successes, sports successes... and the list goes on and on. It can feel like a dog-eat-dog world on that soccer field of parenthood.

This competitive culture and a lack of true community and connection lowers our dopamine levels, so we temporarily remedy the situation in a distracting way by seeking a dopamine hit. This absolutely affects how we feel about ourselves, and it affects how our children experience us in the aftermath of this cycle.

An antidote to this cycle is to begin engaging authentically with your kids as a conscious parent, which we started addressing in the last chapter. That looks different for all of us. For many of us, it involves engaging in a *not-so-social media-post-worthy* way. Your kids really just want to know and spend time with the real you.

The authentic me swears way more frequently than my children would like me to. They have taken it upon themselves to take a stand for a better way to communicate than using curse words to get a point across. They love to point this out to me, and it makes for funny role-reversal banter between us. Over the years, I have toned down my inner truck driver, but I con-tinue to be a bit foul-mouthed and uncensored. In doing so, I am with my kids more as my real self. This is the point of authentic engagement. We interact more frequently with our kids by unapologetically sharing our whole selves, and this creates a solid foundation for a connected relationship. Don't you want to really know your children and feel comfortable allowing them to really know you? You can lead the way (even though it may not look how you think the world's greatest mom should look). My point is that you don't need to be the world's greatest mom... just the *real deal* in your kids' eyes.

Journal to uncover the "thing" that you are doing to feel better, and to identify what circumstances or behaviors bring on distraction episodes for you. Begin to look for patterns so you can learn what sends you into a downward spiral and causes you to turn to your coping strategy to feel better. Remind yourself that you are human and just looking for a way to reduce the bad emotions. Beating yourself up will stunt your growth. Focus on awareness and acceptance. As you find your patterns, possibly the same ones your parents used, you can begin to practice more positive parenting methods. Repeated practice of new parenting tools and concepts will develop healthier parenting patterns that you will pass down to your children, grandkids and beyond. The hardest part is taking the time to learn different methods from the the way most of us were raised. The old model used a lot of fear, punishment and threats because it was based on the belief that humans would inherently choose a selfish, unkind and irresponsible path if left to our own innate motivations. We now know that is a bunch of crap and the opposite is actually true. Humans are wired for positive connections and little kids specifically want to please the leaders of their tribe or family. This is primal wiring within the human brain that can be traced back to our ancestors. Think about certain breeds of dogs and how some tend to be swimmers or herders. If you trace back to the roots of certain breeds you will find a specific explanation unlocking the original purpose of those traits. Perhaps that breed was traditionally used by shepherds to assist in herding sheep. The primitive wiring for herding can still be observed many generations later in Border Collie's for example, even though in today's world, most Border Collie's are suburban house dogs as opposed to living on a sheep herding farm. Similarly, humans have leftover wiring within our brains that affects our behavior like craving deep connected relationships with the people that reside in our caves. Otherwise known as the family unit in modern terms. As a skeptic myself, I just love a theory backed by science.

I believe that it doesn't need to take months or years to learn the new and improved positive parenting methods, and luckily, our kids provide tons of opportunities to practice what we learn. Repetition builds mastery and all you need to do is get started. I teach a great step one course called Conscious Parent Mastery (http://www.randirubenstein.com/a-parent-academy-conscious-parent-mastery/) to begin changing your family legacy in six short weeks. There are many great positive parenting courses out there and the most important thing is to find an instructor that appeals to you and get started.

CONSCIOUS PARENTING TOOL: GREEN HABITS

Now that you understand some of the science behind your need for that distraction that helps you to feel better, it hopefully makes sense why a replacement dopamine-increasing strategy is the way to go. I refer to healthy replacements as green habits. For me, this term encompasses healthy activities like doing yoga, exercising, making green drinks, and practicing meditation. My belief is that substituting some of these green concepts for your old, unhealthy patterns can provide the relief you were looking for with your original go-to distraction methods, and leave you feeling so much better.

If you really want to be a conscious parent who is present more often than not, and more in the moment with your kiddos, it is important to set yourself up for success. To kick your distraction habit of binge eating, screen time, excessive working, smoking, drinking, online shopping, etc., a new habit will help to set you up for success. In addition to feeling at peace when your head hits the pillow at night, your body will look and feel better. And isn't that desire to feel better what got you into this mess in the first place? You just wanted to feel better... even just for a sec.

The alternative habits listed below have been extremely helpful in my life. As someone with an addiction-prone brain, my methods for coping with feelings of discomfort in my life have typically been unhealthy. I try to incorporate the activities listed below in my life on a regular basis. Some weeks are more successful than others. What I can tell you is that when I stay the green course more often than not, I see and feel the results and it builds forward momentum. The most important thing for me has been to get back on the horse when I fall off, to start again rather than giving up and beating myself up for knowing better and not doing better. Usually, it is as simple as getting my tush to a yoga class, drinking a fresh green juice, and taking my dogs for a walk while listening to something motivational. My point is that the goal is not to live a perfectly green life, but to use green tools as a healthy alternative to support yourself on your quest to feel good, so you can show up for yourself and for the people you love.

The Habit of Tapping

Tapping is also called EFT, which stands for Emotional Freedom Technique. Tapping is an amazing tool that can provide relief that's similar to the effects of acupuncture. However, it doesn't involve needles, and you can do it on yourself. Tapping consists of tapping on the end points of the meridians, or energy pathways, of your body. The research supporting this healing modality teaches that it is a way to retrain the deep survival part of your prehistoric reptilian brain from being fired into a state of fight-or-flight when it's not necessary.

Have you ever wondered why you can't stop certain self-destructive patterns that you use to numb or feel better? Why do you continue to binge eat when you are alone or stressed, even though that extra 20 pounds is negatively affecting your self-esteem and life in big ways?

It turns out that the body stores negative energy about issues where you feel powerless. I have heard this described as, "The issues are in our tissues." Unfortunately, I can't remember who coined this catchy phrase. I'm sure I heard it while listening to an inspiring podcast on my iPhone while on a dog walk or shopping for groceries. I really live by these dorky, I mean green, methods.

Tapping serves as a replacement coping mechanism to use when something triggers you, instead of using your typical method of distraction. Honestly, the hardest part is becoming aware in a stressful moment and choosing to tap rather than stress eat or whatever coping strategy you typically use to distract yourself from the difficult feelings.

Nick Ortner, the tapping guru, has loads of resources, including books and videos, that are easily accessible on the Internet. The tapping technique is easy to learn and to practice throughout your day to support you in bringing new, healthier patterns in to your life. You can find out more about it at http://www.tappingsolutionfoundation.org/howdoesitwork/.

The Habit and Practice of Yoga

Okay, so full disclosure: when it comes to yoga, I can be described as a pusher. Yoga is one of the healthiest and most rewarding habits I have adopted, and I have been known to push it on resistant people. As a chocolate-cake-sharer, I want to give each and every one of you a fork, or, in this case, a mat.

Even though I would like to say I'm a full-fledged yogi, my appreciation for yoga began because it combines exercise with an effective replacement for cigarette addiction. Yoga has become a regular practice for me and, yes, I think I will be a student forever.

As I continuously peel back the layers of the yogic onion, I feel like the yoga practice that began for me as a green replacement habit is a rich metaphor for my life off the mat and outside the yoga room. I didn't set out to do yoga for that outcome, and I'm almost hesitant to share it with you now, because it sounds like the exact type of reasoning that would have sent me running in the opposite direction when I was a beginner. In fact, I tried several yoga classes and studios before I got the bug. Many of those classes didn't fulfill me in the way I was hoping. I had several yoga experiences where I felt like the words of the instructor didn't match the energy of the people at the studio. There was so much talk of "love, light, and namaste," and yet I felt those terrible feelings of "compare and despair" as I tried to learn the breathing and do the awkward poses, and as my inflexible body seemed to refuse to comply and contort. I felt like I was surrounded by a bunch of unfriendly people who were in far better physical condition than I was, and who were showing off all their cool yoga moves and acrobatics. I now know that, yes, there was some of that, *and* I was in a much less clear and confident place myself, so I was projecting my internal state. Seven years later, my experience with yoga is that my favorite yoga instructors and studio and fellow students bring community, warmth, and support into my life. I always leave a yoga class in a better place than I was when I went in.

To truly practice yoga as it was intended, the primary focus is on the inhale and the exhale. Yoga can be viewed as a metaphor for life in that life begins on an inhale and ends on an exhale. I have also heard smoking described similarly. Even though most smokers would never choose such a filthy, disgusting habit, on top of the actual physical addiction to nicotine there may be a subconscious addiction to the meditative components of the inhale/exhale piece. I think this is true for me. Thank goodness that, for our kids, the smoking smear campaign has been effective, and the act of smoking has become the equivalent of wearing a Scarlet Letter in this day and age. For those of us who struggle with the love/hate smoking relationship, there is a lot of shame and secrecy involved. We *know* better. Yet, many well-educated and health-conscious people who live their lives "knowing better" continue to be drawn in by the inhales and the exhales associated with smoking.

For me, yoga keeps me in shape and has served as a replacement addiction, because it feels meditative and relaxing to my body, much like the act of smoking did. And, obviously, yoga brings a ton of amazing side effects.

The Habit of Green Drinks

Apparently, drinking green stuff has become a movement—and it may give you one (sorry, I just couldn't refuse the opportunity for a little crude humor). The green smoothie and green juice movement is happening, with many folks choosing to drink valuable nutrients, in addition to eating salads and veggies to feed their bodies.

I would rather drink my greens than eat them. I eat salads and veggies, but deep down I'm a burger-and-fries girl. I am not an expert at making green drinks, although I do throw in a handful of spinach or kale in my smoothies at home. My kids resist green smoothies, but I am sometimes successful at sneaking in green stuff when I mask it in a chocolate banana smoothie. I swear, it tastes like a Wendy's Frosty. I try to drink a green drink every day, and I literally feel an energy surge after a green juice. My favorite combination is orange, grapefruit, spinach, kale, and basil.

The Habit of Walking Outside

I love walking outside with my dogs. Oftentimes I drag along my husband and kids. I find that walking is beautifully conducive to having a productive convo with your peeps. There is something about walking side by side, without direct eye contact, that seems to be the equivalent of truth serum for my kiddos—especially my teenagers. And when I am feeling bored or lonely—traditionally the moments when I seek unhealthy distractions—walking and listening to something inspirational and motivational provides a supportive habit replacement for me.

Life today involves many entertainment choices, due to all the access we have to technology. I used to spend many hours gabbing on the phone, with an underlying intention to connect with a friend but, ultimately, wasting lots of time gossiping and then feeling drained. I replaced that activity with getting fresh air by walking and listening to something motivating, educational, and/or funny on my phone. The fresh air, increased breathing, and movement of my body while my mind is being inspired gives me more energy and has been effective during times when I would have turned to distracting behaviors as a means to fill a void in my day.

What do you turn to in moments of boredom, loneliness, or stress? Is it shopping for stuff you don't need? Binge watching? Gossiping? Eating? The Facebook newsfeed time suck? Why not try taking a walk—by yourself or with someone you want to connect to—and see how that feels?

The Habit of Conscious Breathing

Conscious breathing helps combat yelling behavior. You know those times, the ones most of us have had, when you find yourself slamming your kids with harsh words said in an angry tone because they said or did something disrespectful or crappy. Of course there are a million and one ways to justify your outburst. In fact, many other parents will pat you on the back for showing "them" who's the boss in this era of entitled children—thus, reinforcing the "us vs. them" mentality found in many families between parents and kids. Your behavior seems *warranted* and yet the inevitable tossing and turning layered in guilt and regret consumes your mind later as you attempt to turn off the world and put your exhausted body to bed finally.

Your intense love and strong maternal instincts as a mom are the reasons you feel remorseful for losing your cool even though your kid's behavior was less than stellar as well. Intuitively, you know that yelling at your little cave people won't support the close knit connections your primitive cave brain craves. There is a wide range of words and behavior that comprise the category involving yelling. Apparently, scary facial expressions accompanied by rude words, count as yelling even if your voice isn't technically louder than a whisper according to my kiddos. Yelling is mean. I don't know about you but I dislike people that yell at me or scrunch up their faces and give me looks of disapproval accompanied by insults. Why would it be any different for our kids? It is incredibly confusing for kids to love their parents more than anything and yet not to like us or feel liked by us.

How can we expect to be in positive relationships with our kids if we are constantly losing our cool and possibly even blaming them for our behavior while hurling rude words their way? Breathe to stop yelling. **Humans are the only animals that can actually manipulate our own breath to send our nervous systems the message that we are safe.**

As humans, we can actually avoid the flight, fight, freeze survival responses when we feel our stress hormones kick in due to a triggering situation. Training yourself and your kids to utilize the breath when you feel scared, angry or anxious is literally the gift that will keep on giving. Incorporating deep breathing techniques into your life as a coping mechanism for hard feelings, retrains your brain.

Breathing as a method for stress reduction will lower your tendency to yell by 87%. Okay, I may have made up that percentage but trust me, this breathing stuff works. As a person with an aggressive nature and a childhood involving a decent amount of yelling and tension in the family, it would make sense for me to be a yeller. Replacing the yelling words with deep meditative breaths has been an effective pattern shifter for me personally. In fact, when my kids were little and they heard me taking deep audible breaths, they would immediately ask, "Uh oh. Who's in trouble? Why are you upset?" I consider a little bit of panic at the sound of their mama taking yoga breaths to be a win compared to the damaging effects of going into Mommy Dearest mode.

We know yelling isn't productive. This is why we feel so insanely guilty later. We can justify our adult meltdowns six ways from Sunday because kids FREQUENTLY behave like little creeps—especially kids that are brought up in families where the adults model equally creepy behavior through yelling and using harsh words on a regular basis with the people they love the most in the world. None of it makes sense and yet, most of us continue this pattern if we were raised with this destructive parenting style. This fear based method of controlling kids is deeply ingrained in many of us due to our childhood programming.

How many of us are posting our meltdown moments on social media? There is a reason this is usually closeted behavior. You have received "the call" to raise your kids differently but you haven't learned how to get your kids to listen without resorting to threats, rewards, punishments and sometimes, yelling. You may be saying to yourself, "I would love to be the parent who raises responsible and cooperative kids through positive methods but what exactly does that look like and how do I pull it off on those mornings when no one has their shoes on, the T.V. is blasting and the school tardy bell will be ringing in 5 minutes?". I get it. It's hard to keep it together during these challenging daily encounters.

This dynamic didn't happen on its own and it won't get better on its own either. Change begins with awareness because you have to know what to change to begin changing. You are becoming aware and your first baby step in scenes like the one above is to breathe and do everything in your power to stay calm while successfully getting your people to school without accidentally exacerbating the situation and making it worse. The time to problem solve and come up with a new method is NEVER during the stressful moment. For now, breathe and simply ask how you can help when you find yourself in the middle of one of these situations. Resist the urge to blame and punish. That is no way to separate for the day; sending off your kids prepared to grow their brilliant minds. Yelling and separating with heightened cortisol levels literally negatively affects your kids ability to learn.

Until we actively learn to change, this vicious cycle repeats day after day, year after year, and generation after generation. Trust me. Learn how to take deep breaths and give yourself this gift. It's even free!

You can find out more by searching the Internet for *short breathing methods* and, of course, there is even an iPhone app to assist you with my favorite technique, square or box breathing which can be found at http://boxbreathing.org/.

Using Green Habits with Your Kids

Years ago, when I was a student of the program, Conscious Discipline, the central theme as I understood it was: Adults must walk the walk first before we have any business talking the talk to our kids. In other words, practice what you preach because kids learn by the behavior their parents model rather than the words we use to lecture them. This is also relevant in terms of living a life involving green habits.

If you want your kids to eat healthy, be athletically fit, have body confidence, and respond calmly and rationally when upset rather than having explosive tantrums, then incorporating green habits into BOTH of your lives will support you in achieving these goals.

Often as parents, we have expectations for our kids that we haven't met ourselves. It comes from a good place because we want the world for them. Of course, we don't want our kids to need coping strategies that induce negative side effects in their lives. We know how much of a struggle it has been for us and would never want that for the people we love the most. The best place to start is by spending time together and teaching them some fun child-friendly methods. Incorporate new positive routines during moments when you are getting along. Never try creating new patterns during a power struggle or your child will totally rebel and resent the healthy habits. I teach lots of these methods in my parenting programs. For example, there are breathing techniques specifically geared towards kids that provide a great visual effect and taps into their magical thinking brains. Taking a dog walk together or having a special smoothie P.E.T. date are super-easy pattern disrupters that promote connection. You can incorporate these new green habits into your daily life immediately. These little shifts will provide huge relational dividends between you and your peeps.

* * *

Incorporating green habits that feel good for you into your family culture is a simple choice that can have big results. The ones I listed here are merely recommendations based on things that have enhanced my family and life. I am not a nutritionist or health expert by any means so knock yourself out exploring what works for you.

I believe that it takes forty days to create a new pattern by retraining your brain with a healthier habit. Factoring in an accountability program like forty days of yoga or a six-week parenting program such as, Conscious Parent Mastery (http://www.randirubenstein.com/a-parent-academy -conscious-parent-mastery/) or Close The Parent Gap (http://www.randirubenstein.com/close-the-parent-gap), can help solidify a new healthier pattern. Unfortunately, if all you do is read these words without following up with action steps, it is unlikely that you will change old patterns and create the family culture you are craving.

Transforming your family by creating new healthier patterns takes action. The only way to move forward and begin creating the life and family you deserve is to start with tiny actions. Massive changes taken too quickly and all at once will most likely overwhelm you and you won't keep them up. This is why we typically don't stick to New Year's resolutions.

The good news is that you are taking action by being here with me—right here, right now. You are taking the time to expand your mind and think about the hard stuff rather than running for the hills to distract yourself from the difficult feelings. This counts as your first baby step. Next, find a program or accountability buddy. Each new baby step will reveal itself in due time and as long as you continue consistently moving forward, you will accomplish big things for your family in very little time.

The important thing to understand is that the coping strategy that you have used to feel better has been a source of survival for you. You have not done it because you are a weak person or a bad parent. Shifting those feelings of guilt toward understanding and compassion for yourself is a total game-changer.

As you will learn in Chapter 3, tuning into the protective whispers of your body will be the ultimate green habit and supportive tool in closing *The Parent Gap t*o change unhealthy patterns and possibly change your family legacy.

CHAPTER 3

TUNE INTO YOUR BODY'S WHISPERS

"Just as we can know the ocean because it always tastes of salt, we can recognize enlightenment because it always tastes of freedom."

BUDDHA

SO THIS HAPPENED...

Lucy, a mom of adorable six-year-old twin boys, usually pours her first glass of wine while she prepares a well-balanced dinner for her family. She tells herself she's unwinding with a nice glass of wine after an exhausting and activity-filled day. Lucy's husband is the breadwinner, and she prides herself on taking sole responsibility of their two boys and the daily running of the household. Her husband

61

is a nice guy who would be willing to participate in the household chores and meeting the needs of the boys, but Lucy has trained him to be fairly hands-off. She likes to be in control and she keeps a mental tally of all the ways she is kicking ass and taking names as a "domestic engineer extraordinaire." She loves praise and validation from her husband, and they often bond over the pity they feel for the many hardworking guys who are not being taken care of in the way Lucy takes care of her family.

Lucy begins her day at 5:45 a.m. and gets busy packing lunches, making coffee and hot breakfast for her family, and taking a few moments to check her email and gather her thoughts for the day. At least, that is what she tells herself around midnight the night before, as she sets her alarm for that crack-of-dawn wake-up call that will come way too soon. The truth is, Lucy needs to get up so early because she needs extra morning time to get herself together before her family awakens. She will drink two full cups of coffee and allow herself the required amount of time for the three Advil and the caffeine to take effect, relieving her pounding headache due to lack of sleep combined with the bottle of wine she downed the night before.

Each night, Lucy pushes the plaguing image of the movie *Groundhog Day* out of her mind as she pours that first glass of wine and begins to superficially celebrate all the ways she showed up that day as the World's Greatest Mom, one who deserves to unwind, one who is a legal adult and is allowed to have a simple glass of wine. She manages to stay focused on all the things she accomplished on her to-do list that day involving cooking, shuttling kids to school and soccer practice, playdate coordination, room mom emails, meal planning, shopping and prep, cleaning, and laundry. It won't be until later that night, during her third glass of wine, that she will give in to the moments involving darkness, shame, guilt, and, ultimately, loneliness. As her head pounds the next morning while she waits for the coffee and Advil to kick in, she will make silent promises to begin living differently.

Unfortunately, Lucy's promise to herself will be broken in roughly twelve hours, as she looks for an escape from the deep loneliness she feels on a daily basis. Lucy has become quite a pro at hiding from her true feelings, inner wisdom, and knowing, by pretending to feel fulfilled in her life while she numbs the sensations in her body through functional alcohol dependency. Lately, it has become increasingly more difficult for Lucy to keep up the façade of a perfect life. Each morning as she waits for the effects of the Advil and coffee to kick in, her reality is beginning to feel like one of those lies you told as a teenager that snowballed, and it's just before everything goes South and your parents find out everything.

During the early morning hours, when the world is still so quiet, Lucy enters into a brutally honest conversation with herself and vows to end this cycle. *Today.* This conversation is growing darker and more painful each day as she doesn't actually keep her promise from the day before. She keeps a mental tally of all the evidence that leads her to believe that she is a weak, selfish, and distracted mother who's choosing her love for alcohol over the needs of her family.

Can you relate to Lucy? Many of us have been where Lucy is with one numbing measure or another. If I could tell Lucy something in the midst of her dark thoughts, it would be this: "You are not alone."

Lucy is human. There are things in her life that she is simply resisting feeling. They're just too painful. Alcohol literally numbs her thoughts and the sensations of her body when the silence of the world becomes too loud to bare at night. She busies herself during the daylight hours with errands and activities as she plays the *Super Mom* role but the stillness of evening feels like torture. Lucy has habitually learned to cope with her unfulfilled reality with a nightly bottle of wine as her *go to* method to try and distract herself from the loneliness she feels inside.

If you relate to Lucy, please believe me when I tell you that you are also not alone in this. After having an eating binge or experiencing moments like Lucy had in the early mornings, the original discomfort you were running from actually intensifies as shame and guilt come aboard. This shame spiral that you may have experienced affects many other women as well. This is an unfortunate result of the current female loneliness epidemic, which specifically affects moms, in my opinion. Most of us who distract and feel guilty later because we worry about the effects of our behaviors on our kids, have probably numbed our body sensations for some time. For Lucy, loneliness and disappointment have been too big to feel, and the desire to numb the discomfort has resulted in a dependency on a substance she uses to try and feel better. Ultimately, it only makes her feel worse.

CONSCIOUS PARENTING LESSON AND SKILL: TUNING IN TO YOUR BODY'S PROTECTIVE WHISPERS

What does your body have to do with being a more conscious parent? *Everything.* I am not a professional trained in addiction but as an addiction prone person myself, I have studied, read and thought a lot about addiction. My extremely lay opinion is that those of us prone to addiction happen to be energetically sensitive people. We literally have highly attuned nervous systems and are greatly affected by other people's energy. This is why we tend to be the people that are quite often the first responders during a crisis and the ones that others turn to for help.

We are extremely empathetic and feel other people's pain as if it is our own. It is hard to feel things deeply especially in a *how's the weather* society with a theme song of *Don't Worry Be Happy*. Humans are messy and layered with lots of emotions other than happiness. However, we are taught at a very young age that the darker emotions are not for public display and as energetically sensitive people, we feel all emotions intensely. Therefore, many of us become addicted to ways that help us conceal the dark emotions and the vicious cycle that Lucy finds herself in becomes all too common.

If you have been a classic distractor as a means to dull the big emotions, the chances are that your body feels numb. When you numb your body's whispers, you ignore the messages it's sending that are intended to protect you. Your body likes to feel good. When you condition yourself to ignore negative sensations that result from heightened cortisol, by becoming numb, you are refusing to listen to and heed your inner protective mechanism. It is like rejecting Mike Tyson as your bodyguard in a Middle Eastern war zone. Not a smart decision.

Our brains have primitive, instinctive programming that we were born with. Again as you know, certain breeds of dogs are born knowing how to herd or how to hunt rodents? Well, it's kind of like that, as I briefly mentioned earlier. Many experts refer to these instinctive patterns we have as our lizard or reptilian brain. These body whispers are primal instincts within all humans. This is what is being referred to when "survival instincts" are mentioned: our instincts to fight, flee, or freeze when we're in trouble.

Science suggests that when the human brain detects a situation that represents something scary, our hormones fluctuate and we have a physical response. As I briefly discussed earlier, evolution suggests that this was originally a protective measure from our cave-people days, meant to fight off a sudden attack by a wild boar or another super-scary animal while we were out on a hunt. The stress hormone cortisol, in such a situation, would rise dramatically and our adrenaline would kick in, causing us to run faster (flight), or suddenly feel full of energy and stick the boar with a spear (fight), or curl up in a ball and hope the danger passes by without noticing us (freeze).

This primitive brain's role is to guide and protect you. It sends your body signals that create chemical and hormonal shifts and fluctuations. *This results in actual physical sensations.* When you tune in to these body sensations, rather than numbing out with distractions, you will be shocked to discover how difficult it is to go back to ignoring the signals. These are your body whispers, and you will quickly learn that they can help you. Once you experience their level of loyalty and protectiveness, you will never want to turn them off again. They are your secret, protective weapons, to be valued and appreciated.

Learning how to tune in to your body's whispers is the equivalent of telling your Guardian Angel that you are ready to allow her to keep you safe.

For those of us who have created a numb body to protect ourselves from pain and discomfort when we didn't know another way, tuning back in to hearing and feeling our body's whispers can take a little time. The best way is to start by noticing when you are experiencing a trigger—a situation that annoys, frustrates, or angers you. Notice whether your body temperature rises. Do you begin to sweat? Does your heart rate speed up? Begin to be willing to simply feel the intense sensations associated with being triggered, and then notice what your go-to distraction method is to feel better. Try your hardest to do this noticing without judgment.

As you learn to notice your body's whispers, you will begin to identify people, things, and situations that trigger you. The process of understanding what is happening in your life that causes negative sensations in your body will lead you to the root of why you are seeking distracting behaviors to feel better. This is the awareness scavenger hunt that will become your new secret weapon in keeping your cool as a parent and being able to retrain your brain so you can handle tough situations in a way that allows you to feel proud and celebrate yourself.

For example, what parent wants to be described as a yeller? Did it feel good for any of us when our parents lost their tempers? Speaking from experience, I can say that it feels even crappier when that yelling parent is me. When I listen to my body's whispers, I can often resist the urge to react to a triggered situation by yelling. This is an empowering skill that gives you access to a healthier response to lower the stress hormones racing through your system rather than losing your temper.

Noticing your body's sensations and whispers will also help you in making decisions and determining who feels safe and trustworthy for you. When I am in the presence of a frenemy, I am now so practiced at hearing my body's whispers of warning that they sound more like screams. My body temperature will rise and I will sweat like a scared animal in the presence of a predator. I will spare you the weird smell associated with my sweat only during these specific frenemy encounters. It's kinda gross but also kinda cool because it's information that helps me figure out how to handle the situation.

Right now, there is no pressure to get this all at once. What's important for now is simply to do more noticing. Your distractions may still feel like a safe, old friend and, even though it may be embarrassing to admit, it's okay to not be ready to change yet. If you are struggling with addiction of some type that you know, deep down, is going to be impossible to get a handle on by yourself, please reach out for support. Remember that you're a human who's living a human experience, who's often just trying to feel better in a human moment. Change will happen as you release the judgment, experience more self-awareness, begin incorporating the tools I am sharing with you, and reach out for help when you need it.

CONSCIOUS PARENTING TOOL: CAN YOU SPEAK UP?

This tool will teach you how to begin tuning back in to your body's guidance and learn to feel the sensations you have effectively numbed over the years. Depending mostly on the reasons you began to ignore your body's whispers in the first place, you may find that there are a lot of layers to uncover and move through as you move toward hearing your body's whispers. If you have repressed emotions due to childhood trauma, especially sexual abuse, your body is most likely very numb. If that is the case, you may want to get professional support and work toward feeling your body's whispers. You have experienced so much pain already and I beg you to be patient with yourself and treat yourself with kindness and compassion as you learn this life-changing tool. You deserve a Guardian Angel. Give yourself this gift and learn to hear your body's whispers again like you could as a small child.

Can You Speak Up? Exercise

- Close your eyes and picture a time in your life right at the moment that you received bad news.

- Allow yourself to really imagine and be back in that moment.

- Notice the discomfort in your body. Where do you feel it? (head, shoulders, throat, neck, jaw, chest, etc.).

- Give the sensation a name (warm, sharp, tight, etc.).

- That sensation is your body whispering to you. Now that you have allowed yourself to feel the sensation associated with bad news, you will be more likely to notice the sensation—or some version of it—when it speaks to you in little whispers.

- As you begin to hear these whispers, you can ask them to speak up by trying to identify the triggering event. What about the thing you just experienced reminds your brain of a memory from your past? You will be surprised by the way seemingly random memories and intense body sensations reveal themselves as you invite your body's whispers to speak up.

* * *

If your body is consistently experiencing numbness as a result of relying on distractions to avoid negative sensations, hidden beliefs associated with body triggers are much harder to excavate. Tuning in to your body whispers, and learning to listen and become aware of your triggers, will help you uncover your old stories and allow you to lay new ski tracks in your brain and create new patterns for your family.

Courage and curiosity about delving into your history are coming up next. Encourage yourself as you practice being courageous and curious about your story. Keep in mind that your past brought you to this moment in your life. Finding the willingness to curiously delve into your story will put a huge piece of the puzzle into place. Keep reading, Mamacita!

CHAPTER 4

COURAGE AND CURIOSITY

"Tell me a fact and I will learn. Tell me a truth and I will believe. But tell me a story and it will live in my heart forever."

NATIVE AMERICAN WISDOM

SO THIS HAPPENED...

In my family, when I was growing up, we never talked much about our family history, or really about anything other than the immediate experience. I had young parents and, frankly, I always felt a source of pride in that. They were more hip and attractive than many of my friends' parents. My mom was a MILF before that was even a thing, and my dad had those Magnum, P.I/Tom Selleck good looks, but without the creepy child-molester mustache. My parents were not strict and we didn't have a lot of rules. They never looked over my homework, pressured me in a direct way to achieve or perform, and their parenting style could be described as hands-off. Not in a purposely neglectful way; more in an "It's the 1970s" way.

My parents worked, smoked, played bridge, smoked, watched TV, smoked, gambled, smoked... you get the gist. Secretly, I'm a little envious of the way they smoked so openly and freely compared to today with all of the positive peer pressure not to smoke due to the evidence that it will kill us. I have had a love/hate affair with smoking since my teen years even though I hated my parents' smoking as a little kid. Patterns like these frequently repeat, as I have experienced.

My folks loved having us kids around all the time, whether they were enjoying their favorite activities or not. They were not going to alter their behaviors to ones that were more child-centered, but as kids we knew we were always welcome and wanted by them. I always felt extremely loved. When I was young, we often hung out in our parents' bed at night after dinner—playing cards, watching television, eating candy, and smoking. Well, the kids didn't smoke... our parents had *some* sense of responsibility!

We were very close to my Nan, my mom's mom. She moved to South Texas from Miami to live near us. She cooked dinner for us most nights and was a constant presence as I was growing up—often sitting in the recliner in my parents' room as we kids sandwiched in between my bookend parents many evenings in the bed. It was like a modern version of the grandparents from *Charlie and the Chocolate Factory*. Only ours involved cards, candy, and cigarettes.

My other grandmother, my dad's mom, Magda, lived in New Jersey and was not an active presence during my childhood. She and my dad were not close and, until I was eleven, we saw her about once a year. She was a beauty with a thick, Hungarian accent, and I always marveled that my dad understood her and responded to her during conversations.

When I was eleven, my parents had a falling out with Magda during my brother's bar mitzvah weekend. It would be another 17 years until I laid eyes on Magda again.

Fast-forward to November of 2014. My dad and I were spending several hours together at Methodist Hospital in Houston as we waited for those words you long to hear when someone you love is in surgery: "We got it all. She's resting and doing great." My mom was undergoing her second reconstructive surgery after having been diagnosed with very early stage breast cancer six months earlier.

Even though my dad is a constant fixture in my family's life, it is rare that we sit and hang out alone for more than ten minutes, much less for three hours—side by side, with no buffers. I sensed a slight bit of nervousness from my dad as we waited together during my mom's surgery.

My family knows about my coaching practice, and I'm pretty sure they worry that at any given moment there is the potential for me to launch into "self-help mumbo jumbo." Needless to say, that is not their comfort zone. Any talk about the past, feelings, or—God forbid—my "journey" can cause any one of them to break out into hives and run for the hills in need of an emergency cigarette break.

I can't say I was entirely comfortable myself as I sat there with my dad. Usually we have the kids to distract us and to bond over. My dad is the only person I can sit with while we watch and discuss my children ad nauseam. Even my husband tires of this activity, and they are his kids! I, on the other hand, have had a borderline addiction or obsession with these three little (and now not so little) beings that came out of my body. Well, my dad has the same addiction/obsession with my children. We also both tend to be topic-dwellers who can tell the same story over and over again. When alone, we both, unselfconsciously, repeat kid story after story, especially when there are no witnesses to point out how annoying we are being.

So, during the first two hours of our wait, we did exactly that. We discussed uneventful stories and observations about my kids that would have bored anyone else to tears.

We also looked at recent pictures of my kids on my phone and reveled in our shared adoration of them. And then the awkward silence rained down upon us.

So I took a leap of faith and decided to bring up a topic rarely discussed: his mother, Magda.

Let me back up to explain my sudden curiosity about the Magda story. My daughter, who was 13 years old at the time, had recently come home and told me she was learning in school about the Holocaust. I was surprised when she began discussing some of the most shocking details, which involved the quick elimination of most of the Hungarian Jewish population, toward the end of the war. She was surprised when I told her that she was one-quarter Hungarian Jew herself. She'd had no idea, because Magda had not been a part of our lives. She immediately began inquiring about Magda's story and how she could have survived. I didn't have the answers to her questions. We had always known that Magda was a Holocaust survivor and that my dad and his brother had been born in a displaced persons camp in Germany just after the war. We knew Magda had been in Auschwitz-Birkenau, the camp built specifically for mass extermination. We kind of remembered that she was the sole survivor of her family. We basically knew nothing else.

Initially, my dad became defensive and tried to talk me out of my curiosity. He used some aggressive mannerisms and his go-to deterrent tactic that sounds something like, "Randi, why are you always trying to dig up the past and things that no one has any interest in talking about? It's not important. It doesn't affect us now. Who cares. Forget about it. She is a miserable, evil witch. There is no reason to waste our breath talking about her."

But instead of resorting to my old strategies involving a similarly aggressive skill set, or letting the topic go, I reached into my coaching bag of tricks and tried a different, more compassionate approach.

I said, "Dad, do you realize that it is a miracle that we are here. You, me, our family... my kids. We are all miracles. We were never meant to be, according to Hitler's plan. Our ancestors were basically exterminated... all except one. Magda. She has lived a bitter, miserable life. She lived with pain that we can never fully understand. That is probably the reason she tortured you and your brothers. I know it's hard to be curious about her, let alone compassionate, but this is rich history and it's ours. This story is what captivating movies and best-selling novels are made of, and it is actually our story about our ancestors—not only yours. Aren't you the slightest bit curious to discover it before it is too late to celebrate the true miracle behind our existence? Think about it— from Nazi Germany to Houston, Texas, surrounded by your wife, three children, four grandchildren, and having lived an extraordinary life. Your life is truly a miracle."

After that presentation, my dad became much more willing to discuss the life of his mother, who he described as "a more violent version of Mommy Dearest." Subsequently, in the weeks following that waiting room conversation, we did end up finding out many of the horrific details of her Holocaust nightmare and our family history, through the videos of interviews with Holocaust survivors, which we discovered and retrieved through Steven Spielberg's USC Shoah Foundation. The interviews with Magda were extremely difficult to watch, and the details of what happened are worthy of a book in itself.

Also, coincidentally or not, Magda died about two months before this book would be published. She lived alone, without family nearby, in a nursing home in Florida. She had been estranged from two of her five sons and had minimal relationships with the other three at the time of her death.

I believe that Magda may never have spoken of the horrors she endured during the war, but she lived another 73 years wearing those wounds on the outside of her heart. By never discussing or processing her pain, she continuously inflicted it upon her children during their childhoods. Her life was tragic in every way imaginable, in my opinion. I believe that uncovering her Shoah Foundation interviews helped me to understand the roots of many of the unhealthy patterns that I experienced growing up and have been working hard not to pass down to my kids.

The underlying pain and anger that Magda never seemed to process was a constant visitor during my dad's childhood and, to a lesser extent, during mine as well. It is extremely stressful to live in a "walking on eggshells" home, where explosive tempers linger around every corner. Even though my dad may never truly forgive his mother, I think he has experienced some relief by remembering, learning, processing, and shifting his perspective from the wounded child to believing he is a living miracle. This is an example of healing past generations through our cur-rent path. How much better does that feel?

CONSCIOUS PARENTING LESSON AND SKILL: THE PERSPECTIVE SHIFT

What is the perspective shift and why is it important as a parenting skill? Uncovering the stories from your past helps to shift your perspective and to embrace one that feels less painful. We are all on a quest to increase our dopamine levels and feel better. It's part of the human experience and what we strive for—simply to feel good, content, and at peace. The perspective shift is a strategy that will help you feel better.

For example, my dad initially shut down regarding uncovering the details of Magda's Holocaust experience, because the story he was telling himself was that she was a mean, hateful witch. Period. He believed she was a bad person and undeserving of our time, attention, and curiosity. As I chipped away at that deeply held belief by offering a replacement thought—the "we are miracles" story—his perspective shifted, almost instantaneously, from that of a wounded and abused child to that of a 70-year-old adult man whose life is miraculous. He was unaware that this healing was happening, but it was pretty obvious as I saw his face light up and he appeared energized when I offered the new thought focused on the miracle of his life.

As humans, we are wired for story. Stories help us make sense of our lives. Do you remember begging your parents for just one more book? Or, in my case, hiding under the covers with a flashlight until all hours of the night reading Judy Blume or Beverly Cleary?

The most interesting story we will ever learn is the one about our own lives. However, most of us secretly worry that getting curious about our past will be the equivalent of opening up Pandora's box—and that feels super scary. It takes courage to stop running from your history and become willing to "go there." Putting those puzzle pieces together—not from a place of blaming all that should have been different, but from a place of accepting the reality of what is—allows the perspective shift to occur.

When you start embracing your story from a place of adult curiosity rather than continuing to see it from a hurt-childhood perspective, it's incredibly healing, no matter what age you are. Even if you're 70.

Your story becomes like that book you mourn the ending of, even before you read the final page, because you know it has been your best friend for the last week or so and you aren't ready to say goodbye yet. The book of your life always has another chapter, or a prequel that you missed because the memory hadn't resurfaced yet.

CONSCIOUS PARENTING TOOL: STRENGTHENING YOUR PERSPECTIVE-SHIFTING MUSCLE & THE PRODUCTIVE CONVO

Learning to live as a person who considers other people's perspectives can feel like a gift. Shifting your perspective is a continual work in progress, as I can attest. I strive to see another possibility, especially when I am triggered and find myself swirling with negative thoughts, sensations, and emotions.

Think about all the times it has felt like someone's hurtful behavior was intentionally spiteful or malicious toward you. The more I learn, the more I have come to believe that it is almost never actually that. It is almost always about them. This doesn't mean that I continue to stay in the line of fire when I feel dumped on by another person's unresolved business. But understanding their perspective and the fact that it really isn't about me allows me to draw boundaries with empathetic intentions, protect myself, and move on without harboring a bunch of resentment and negativity.

Kids are born egocentric. It is literally developmentally appropriate for our kids to put numero uno first. I point this out because I think it's incredibly important to understand this biological fact. The egocentricity can be traced back to the primitive part of the brain as a survival mechanism. Think about it. When we were cave dwellers, kids were not safe out in the bush unless they were protected by their cave parents. Obviously, there were times they were alone and it was literally life threatening for them. Being self-consumed and self-focused was an instinctual protection for kids. It is completely developmentally appropriate during childhood.

The way kids learn how to be unselfish team players is by being surrounded by empathetic team playing parents leading the family team. Remember, kids learn by watching us rather than listening to all our lectures. I often tell parents that it's easy to make a situation worse by attaching adult meaning to your kid's developmentally appropriate behaviors.

Here's an example scenario to learn about the perspective shift: Your 7-year old son constantly hurts his younger siblings whenever they enter his room and touch his prized *stuff*. You know how boys can be regarding their treasured possessions on the bookshelves in their rooms. You have tried reasoning and pointing out that his younger sibs are just curious and want to be wherever he is because they think he's the coolest. He becomes argumentative and literally refuses to engage in a conversation about this let alone accept ownership for his wrongdoings or show remorse for physically hurting the little people that he is *supposed* to love and protect! Isn't that the traditional role of the big brother? Your brain spins and your blood begins to boil during these moments especially when your younger children are delivered to you "bloodied" emotionally and physically. It appears to the naked eye that your oldest son not only has no biological desire to protect his younger siblings but he shows no signs of remorse or empathy for hurting them. You worry that he might be a narcissist or a sociopath! During these times, you often find yourself yelling, punishing and lecturing upon deaf ears about knowing better, being twice her age and being a selfish bad person. And yet the cycle continues and you're starting to feel like you have to be with your kids at all times to keep the younger ones safe amongst a potential future serial killer!

Applying the perspective shift to have a productive convo with your kids: Your 7-year old is egocentric as 7 year olds have been since the beginning of mankind. His primitive brain sees his room as his cave. His stuff within his cave is precious and valuable to him. These are all the belongings he has in the world. As your younger daughter arrives in your arms "bloodied and beaten", it's important to give her first aid through hugs and healing before you address the 7-year old. This sends your children the message that you value healing over hurting. When you go on the manhunt to take down the 7-year old aggressor before you've addressed your wounded little girl, you channel your attention towards the hurter.

What you focus your attention on grows larger. Therefore, it reinforces the aggressive hurtful behavior when you attend to the aggressor or hurter first. Instead, focus your attention on healing those that are wounded back to optimal health with hugs, empathy and first aid. Then when you are ready to deal with your 7-year old, the conversation will come from a calm centered space now that you understand his perspective through understanding that his primal cave instincts were triggered causing him to react by using the survival instinct of fight. Please don't confuse understanding with condoning. Understanding your son's perspective allows you to think clearly and respond in a productive way, thus teaching him that you don't condone his violent behavior and what to do next time instead.

The productive convo teaches kids a better way and improves future behavior where lectures and punishments sabotage connection and actually reinforce future misbehaviors. A productive convo in this scenario would go something like this: "It seems that your sister came into your room and you weren't happy about that. Something happened and she came to my room with a red mark on her arm and tears on her face. I want to understand your side of the story so we can work together to prevent this from happening again in the future. This family is a team and violence is absolutely unacceptable. I know you follow rules and something must have really upset you for you to act in this way. Tell me about it so we can be a family team and work together to establish rules for entering each other's rooms, touching other family member's possessions and respecting personal space. And just to be clear before we proceed, laying hands on another or using violence is never an option. Got it." Next, you turn to your daughter and say, "Now say to your brother, "You may not hit me and hurt me. Hitting is wrong and it hurts." Address your son, "Say to your sister, I'm sorry I hurt you. I won't do it again." Shake hands and now we are all clear on this important family rule.

* * *

Once you have found the courage to get curious about your history by looking at your parent's stories, you can practice and strengthen your perspective-shifting muscle, experience healing from old wounds and as a result have multitudes of productive convos with your kids. Productive convos are the major building block in the foundation of your connected family unit.

Next, you will add to your new skills to truly excavate the stories and look for negative patterns associated with the pain from those stories. This is not Pandora's box. This part is really fun. Okay, it may not be so much fun at the very beginning, but you now have the courage to get curious and, trust me, it will become empowering and captivating to put the puzzle pieces of your story together.

Buckle up, because this roller coaster ride down memory lane can be a little scary, a lot invigorating, very rewarding, and totally worth it.

CHAPTER 5

EXCAVATING OLD STORIES AND PATTERNS

"Pay close attention to the particular thoughts you use to deprive yourself of happiness."

BYRON KATIE

SO THIS HAPPENED...

Maggie, a 50-ish mother of a 15-year-old daughter, a successful business consultant, an avid volunteer, a devoted wife, and a loyal friend, has an amazingly positive outlook on life. She is the perfect blend of traditionally feminine and masculine characteristics. She is kind, loving, and maternal while also being pragmatic, strategic, and a real go-getter in terms of getting the job done... whatever the job may be at the moment. Working with her as a coach feels the way I have heard teachers describe the ease of working with gifted students. She is a quick study and easily embraces a new tool or a new way of looking at a situation. When it comes to building a more connected relationship with her daughter, she combines her pragmatic consultant's approach with her deep motherly love and her desire to nurture in every situation. The results have been so rewarding for her to experience, and for me to observe, over the course of our working relationship.

Maggie began my eight-week program, *Becoming the Mother You Wish You Had,* which is intended for women with abusive mothers and was inspired by Magda, my dad's mom. Based on Maggie's enthusiasm and star student status, I expected her to soar through the program. One of the first pieces of the program involves digging up the roots of your relationship with your mother. There were a few homework assignments. Maggie, my super star student, missed the deadlines.

Maggie and I hopped on the phone and decided to talk out the assignment. She had convinced herself that she had legitimate things going on that were causing her to blow off the homework. But I suspected she was subconsciously avoiding the assignment and experiencing resistance to the topic. With some gentle guidance, she was able to begin to get slightly curious about her mother's story, though her resistance remained.

I explained to Maggie that there must be some limiting beliefs holding her back that we could excavate if she was truly committed to receiving the benefits of this program. A belief is simply a thought that you have had over and over so many times that it has become a deeply embedded neural pathway or a worn-in "ski track" in your brain. The belief becomes so ingrained that you believe it to be the truth. The painful belief limits the expansion of your mind and your growth.

As we talked about a few of Maggie's memories, stories, and facts about her mother's history, my star student began to get more curious... much like you did when you were a child and all you wanted was one more story from your parent before bed. As the curiosity grew, I noticed that she kept saying, "She didn't even try." I asked what she meant by that and she said, "Well, she didn't even try to improve herself. She studied psychology in college. My mom had smart friends and advisors who were much wiser and more supportive than she was, so there was evidence that my mother surrounded herself with many resources. She had a job for a few years when I was a young teen that involved working with adolescents within our community, and they all loved her. She shared the fake good side of herself with everyone else. But with me, she was critical, negative, and unsupportive. She didn't even try to be a better mother and person for me, even though there was clear evidence that she knew better. She didn't try to be a better mother."

After turning the thought around and discovering evidence that supported a new, less painful thought, Maggie felt tremendous relief and understanding. Uncovering her mother's story included seeing evidence that she had been a fairly broken person who attempted to live vicariously through her daughter because of her own low self-esteem and insecurity. We also felt that Maggie's mother possibly valued superficial wealth and achievement, because those things represented safety in her mind, since her childhood had involved being raised by a single mother and dealing with financial struggles. Maggie's replacement thought was, "Her thinking made her incapable of trying to be a better mother."

Old ski tracks—neural pathways—exist deep within your brain. For pattern-seeking humans, it takes practice to make deep grooves to create new neural pathways. Naming the new story or thought something goofy or fun is really helpful, because the brain and body love to laugh and smile. During a triggered moment, you will be more likely to remember the newer ski track rather than automatically resorting to the old one if it's called something like "pregnancy nightmare," or if the tune "Xanadu" pops into your head as you envision Olivia Newton John in her awesome get-up. This strategy deepens the new ski tracks, resulting in retraining your brain and allowing a new pattern to emerge when you are stuck in a painful belief.

Being a no-nonsense businesswoman, Maggie was quick to point out after the exercise that she enjoyed it, but was not sure of the point since her mother is deceased and she rarely speaks about her. I explained that limiting beliefs embed themselves in our habitual mindsets and affect our lives any time our brains are even remotely reminded of something similar. An activated trigger causes you to feel worked up. When one of your triggers is activated your heart may begin to race and your body temperature rises. You will feel emotions like anger, fear, annoyance, frustration, or sadness, to name a few. Maggie, the A+ student, didn't disappoint. She immediately made a correlation between her husband's frequent "glass is half empty" pessimistic approach to life and how triggering it is for her because it reminds her brain of her mother's constant negativity.

Maggie was excited to begin reinforcing the new ski track of "Her thinking made her incapable of trying." In her head, every time she felt her blood begin to boil when negativity came her way, she would remind herself of the new thought. She knew her hubby would provide ample opportunities for practicing.

CONSCIOUS PARENTING LESSON AND SKILL: THOUGHTS DETERMINE RESULTS

Check out the following illustration. Understanding our thoughts and connecting the dots between thoughts and results is a high-level thinking skill and tool, in my opinion. It has taken me a decent amount of time to truly "get" this conceptually. If the concept sounds like Greek to you, don't worry, I'm no genius, so if I can get it, so can you. Once you learn that your thoughts directly impact your results, this will be a superpower for you, too.

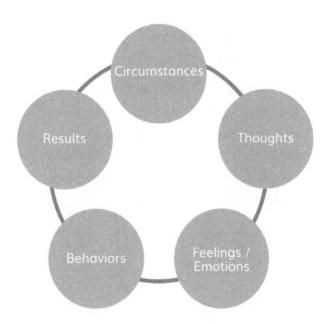

How is this thought model relevant to being a conscious parent? The thought model represents how your thinking affects the way you behave and, ultimately, your results in life.

The action depicted by the diagram moves in clockwise steps. When you find yourself in a particular circumstance (the top circle in the diagram) that triggers a negative feeling, it's because something in that circumstance you are experiencing reminds your brain of a similar experience. The area of the brain that does this controls your survival response—the reaction that causes you to fight, flee, or freeze in the face of danger.

Your current experience does not need to be identical to the original circumstance to trigger your brain and set off a survival response. Your brain does not register the difference between the current triggering experience and the memory. Your body responds to the cortisol surge and, before you know it, subconscious thoughts associated with the old memory come online. This can cause feelings of discomfort resulting in yelling, losing your temper, and feeling guilt, as well as searching for distracting ways to try and feel better. The deeply held belief affects your behavior and determines your results. The bottom line is: your thoughts determine the re-sults you're getting.

The human brain naturally seeks patterns. According to cellular biologist Dr. Bruce Lipton, in the first seven years of life, our subconscious or habitual mind is programmed by the people and behaviors we are surrounded by. They are usually our parents, siblings, teachers, and community. This programming affects the part of your mind that is your automatic default approximately 95 percent of the time, typically. Even though you may read books and seek knowledge to change your life and create new patterns that are different from those you grew up with, it is only about five percent of the time that you tap into that new information located in your conscious brain file cabinet. A thought that you have had over and over, especially one that resulted from an unhappy experience as a young child, has become a deeply ingrained belief and a system of thoughts that you don't even realize you're having. That becomes part of your narrative and you believe it to be true.

If the belief is negative or self-sabotaging, it is referred to as a *limiting belief,* because it limits your ability to grow, heal, and evolve. A limiting belief can be deeply ingrained and very difficult to even identify.

Excavating the *story* connected to a limiting belief is exciting and powerful because once you do so, you can literally create new neural pathways or lay new ski tracks within your brain. The goal is to create new thought patterns that feel much better than the old ones you are ready to kick to the curb.

Once you've successfully uncovered the old, hidden, limiting beliefs, you change the pattern by finding replacement thoughts that feel better. I have done this in my own life and have assisted many clients in accomplishing this work as well. It is a very exciting and cutting-edge approach to change and it feels a little bit like magic. No, I'm not a magician and this is not hocus-pocus, but it is pretty freaking cool how effective thought-dissolving exercises can be, and it amazes me that a coach and regular mom like me, someone without a PhD in neuroscience or some other impressive discipline, can learn this skill so easily. I can lay new ski tracks, retrain my brain, and teach you how to do it, too.

This is how you keep your childhood programming from running the show in your adult life to assist yourself in closing *The Parent Gap* to be a calm and centered parent even during the hard moments with your kids. This is about truly becoming the leader in your own life, and choosing the way you want to raise your kids rather than operating unintentionally on autopilot and allowing the old programming to be the boss and continue to accidentally pass down patterns that never felt good for you in the first place. What's that definition of insanity—expecting different results from the same repeated behavior? Wouldn't you like to live by following a sane model instead?

I won't lie to you. This is a marathon, not a sprint. Thought-dissolving and laying new neural ski tracks takes time, practice, and repetition to build mastery. There are many brain-retraining methods available for transforming painful thoughts. The ones I recommend are the methods of Byron Katie (http://thework.com/en) combined with an approach that involves naming the story.

CONSCIOUS PARENTING TOOL: TRUE STORY OR FABLE?

Are your thoughts true stories you are telling yourself or torturous, painful fables? Painful thoughts or limiting beliefs usually begin to wiggle and feel less true as you spell them out and break them down. As that happens, new, less painful replacement thoughts will emerge.

How to play the game True Story or Fable?:

- The next time you are triggered by a situation where you feel angry, frustrated, annoyed, or find yourself mentally blaming other people for your emotions, notice that you're doing so.

- Play the game: Ask yourself a series of questions to explore whether your thought is true. As you uncover the negative thoughts going through your mind, label each thought as either a true story or a fable.

- Any challenging question you ask about your thought that doesn't get an answer that it is 100% true means that thought is a fable.

An example of the True Story or Fable? game:

Your sister-in-law texts you an hour before her family of six is due to arrive for dinner: *We can't make it.* You feel your heart begin to beat faster and your body temperature rises. You've been to the grocery store and devoted a good portion of your day to making a company-worthy meal, as opposed to a typical edible-enough meal for when there are no guests. Your mind immediately begins swirling with thoughts like these: *She doesn't respect my time. She is so selfish. She thinks the world starts and stops with her family, and she couldn't give a shit about mine. She is disrespectful and doesn't like me and this is her passive-aggressive way of letting me know we are an afterthought.*

You go to the bedroom and close the door and play the True Story or Fable? game, like this:

- *She doesn't respect my time: Can I know this 100 percent for certain? The answer is no. I can't know this with absolute certainty. So this thought is a **fable**.*

- *She is so selfish: She definitely does a lot for her kids, and she's actually a great present-giver. So this thought is a **fable**.*

- *She thinks the world starts and stops with her family, and she couldn't give a shit about mine:* I don't know this for sure. And she actually has done some nice and considerate things for us in the past. So this thought is a **fable**.

- *She is disrespectful and doesn't like me and this is her passive-aggressive way of letting me know we are an afterthought:* Then why would she have said yes in the first place? So this thought is a **fable**.

Next, incorporate the perspective shift, as you learned to do in Chapter 4, to replace the hurtful story with one that feels better: Well, she does have four kids in three different schools, and they're involved in multiple sports and other activities. And it's a school night, so there's homework to oversee. Maybe she is doing all she can to stay afloat. Maybe she had a human moment and had forgotten about something else that was pressing. I mean, I only have three kids and I'm always worried that important things will fall through the cracks. Plus, she doesn't really cook, so she might not realize all the work I put into preparing dinner for six extra people. I doubt she was being malicious. Maybe just a little self-consumed and inconsiderate.

In the above example, even though the negative thoughts have not necessarily become positive thoughts, the painful beliefs begin to wiggle and lift. This shifts those old thoughts from being about you not being worthy of respect, and more toward your sister-in-law and her possible self-involvement due to overwhelm. Doesn't that feel less painful than the original thoughts?

Believing the fables causes us to behave in either aggressive or passive-aggressive ways. Obviously, this then directly affects the health of our relationships. We get those results.

Living stuck in negative or painful thoughts is a way of life for many of us parents. This directly affects how we behave and, of course, it affects our children. When life happens and you become triggered as a hiccup enters your day and throws you off course, how can you be the conscious, present, and engaged parent you aim to be if you're consumed with anger caused by old ski-track thoughts, by swirling, negative thoughts, beliefs, and stories?

CIRCUMSTANCES-THOUGHTS-FEELINGS-BEHAVIORS-RESULTS

When life throws you a hiccup, metaphorically hold your breath and drink some water up-side down, and remember the thought model: circumstances-thoughts-feelings-behaviors-results. Use the tools you've learned here to stop hiccups from turning your life into a momentary vomitorium consisting of triggered angry outbursts that leave you feeling drained, sick, and depleted—and probably aren't much help with creating healthy connections in your family. Wouldn't it feel better to find a replacement thought that allows acceptance and compassion rather than anger, flared tempers, and guilt for yelling or modeling out-of-control behavior?

You get to dress up as a mad scientist and retrain your own brain to create new, healthier patterns. Over the past 20 years or so, neuroscience has made some life-changing discoveries. With the power of the Internet and modern technology, regular folks like me and you have access to those discoveries. What are you waiting for? Try googling topics like *retrain your brain* or *new thought habits*. There are exciting developments that will literally change the way you think. I'm not calling you old, but it turns out you *can* teach an old dog new tricks.

When you begin to retire the old thoughts and bring in new patterns, it is super important to celebrate yourself. You are doing the work. You are changing unhealthy patterns in your life and family. You are healing past, present, and future generations. *That* is pretty freaking awesome.

CHAPTER 6

BE YOUR CHEERLEADER, NOT YOUR FEAR LEADER

"Surround yourself with cheerleaders not fear leaders!"

KAREN SALMANSOHN

SO THIS HAPPENED...

Molly is a mother of three kids. Her oldest son is 16 and, to put it not so lightly, he has been a complete handful his whole life. A team of doctors, psychologists, and psychiatrists have been involved in his care since he was about seven, when it became apparent to his mom that she needed professional support to help her with her son. Molly has received multiple suggestions and possibilities from "the experts" about her son's diagnosis and issues, but nothing has ever seemed conclusive. He has been described as extremely aggressive, which probably contributes to his being an exceptionally gifted athlete. His ultra-athleticism has been a major source of pride for Molly's husband, who basically refuses to see his son's development as anything other than typical.

Molly feels that it has fallen solely on her shoulders to understand her son and provide him with the love and support he deserves. Her husband lives in denial, even though there have been many years of proof that Molly's assessment of their oldest son is spot-on. When the tension in their home feels unmanageable due to their son's aggression, Molly's husband becomes filled with anger and blame and sees their son's behavior as intentional and disrespectful—something their son could easily control. They have lived in this vicious cycle for many years, and it has caused a lot of stress in their marriage, as well as in the other relationships in the family.

Molly has been working diligently for 16 years to understand her son, to help her love him for the unique person he was born to be. She has studied, researched, learned tools and strategies, sought professional support on many aspects, spent countless hours, and invested a lot financially to truly support her child. To me, she has had a *no-quit* spirit as a mother. She is driven by unconditional love.

Molly is the supreme example of a Mama Warrior, in my opinion. She has never given up on her child and she has grown immensely over the last 16 years as a mother and a woman. As a result, for the first time in her son's life, he is not just surviving, he is thriving. The two have an unbreakable bond consisting of love, support, and true connection. By all standards imaginable, this is a major success story.

As I spoke to Molly one afternoon amid a group of women, I found it interesting to hear her describe herself as "a typical quitter." She had quit classes, boyfriends, friendships, jobs, projects, etc. She stated her quitter status as if it was an indisputable fact.

We all pointed out her Mama Warrior qualities, based on evidence we'd seen involving her success with her son, but she dismissed our complimentary words and said she felt they were undeserved. I. Was. Not. Having. That.

I explained to Molly that I used to think of myself as a quitter, too, and as a procrastinator—even though I had lots of evidence to the contrary. What helped me begin to see my quitter story as the fable it was, was taking the Kolbe A Index assessment test and combining it with a few other personality type tests. These tools have supported me in understanding and appreciating myself, as the person I was born to be.

The Kolbe A test measures the way you were born to take action when facing a challenge. This has a lot to do with natural temperament. I have heard that natural temperament can be measured in babies as young as a year old. For example, the baby that touches everything will always be a tactile person who uses their sense of touch to help them solve challenging problems.

I learned from my Kolbe scores that I am more dynamic and produce better results if immediacy and a deadline are involved when working on a project. This challenges the relevance of my negative, self-inflicted title of being a procrastinator. I actually do better work two days before something is due versus working on it weeks ahead of time. And as far as being a quitter, I have an ability to sense when something is not a good choice for me, and I quickly alter my course by shifting gears. I've learned that I have an inability to live a life of complacency. The Kolbe test has helped me turn my negative, self-sabotaging thinking to the opposite. Instead of seeing myself as a quitter, I consider my ability to quickly course-correct as a superpower.

As I shared this explanation with Molly, she began to smile. What I wanted Molly to understand was that, typically, 80 percent of our thinking is negative and fear-based. Not good.

Despite the evidence that spoke to the opposite of her being a quitter, based on her sixteen devoted years to her extraordinary son, Molly's thinking about herself was negative. Everyone but Molly could clearly see the reality of her accomplishments.

With the Mama tribe supporting her, Molly was able to begin shifting her thoughts by celebrating her son's success, largely due to her unconditional love and guidance. She began creating new, positive ski tracks to update her story to one that would impact her life with forward action and momentum. Her smile that day was genuine, contagious, and priceless.

Who were *you* naturally born to be? Celebrating the big and small things that you do every day as a mom, friend, wife, and good person, is the antidote to the negative thinking. This is as true for me and Molly as it is for you.

CONSCIOUS PARENTING LESSON AND SKILL: UNDERSTANDING WHO YOU WERE BORN TO BE

What does investigating your natural temperament and learning to focus on strengths have to do with parenting? As you learn about your unique traits, you will begin to respect and celebrate yourself in an entirely new way.

I love personality tests and assessments, especially the Kolbe. My family members have also taken the Kolbe. It has helped me to truly understand and celebrate them and it allows us to work together more effectively as a team, by acknowledging the individual strengths we each bring to the table.

Through celebrating your natural strengths, you will continue to get stronger, more confident, and be that conscious, self-assured parent that all kids desire to have in their corner. Something I've noticed is, the more I learn about myself and my family with these different reports, the more accepting and celebratory I am toward myself and those I love. Okay, before you completely barf all over me, don't worry, I will always be a fellow self-deprecator, to some degree. I am a lover of humor, especially at my own expense, but I used to participate in jokes about myself in a different way than I do now. Today, I can honestly laugh at myself in the way you do when you love someone even more for their quirks and idiosyncrasies.

A big reason to learn to cheer for yourself is that it feels immensely better to love yourself than not. Also, it is really necessary to honor and respect yourself so that others—like your kids—will follow suit. Doesn't it make sense to model the way you want others to treat you? Isn't this what you want for your kids?

You model the behavior you believe you deserve to get from others. When you model that behavior for your kids—and this is especially important for the girl kids—you can have a really positive impact. Our daughters download every behavior we display, whether we realize it or not. What mother's dream doesn't include her daughter feeling empowered, confident, and never struggling with low self-worth? As you learn about yourself and embrace your uniqueness, you will come to believe even more strongly that you are uniquely awesome. My guess is that you are interesting, engaging, hilarious, and more.

Do you see how a shift in your perspective about yourself allows you to show up in your life and family as the fierce and fun Mama Warrior who kicks A and takes names?

CONSCIOUS PARENTING TOOL: DAILY REPORT CARD

This daily report card exercise is a tool that reinforces the concept *what you focus on grows*. So often, as moms, as we lie down with our thoughts after a long day, we review all of the examples, or "evidence," of the ways we failed ourselves and our kids. They play through our minds like a Depends commercial on fast-forward. By focusing instead, as your head hits the pillow, on things you did well during the day, no matter how small or insignificant they seem, you will begin to change that self-destructive pattern and allow your accomplishments to grow.

By acknowledging little celebrations about yourself, you create new neural pathways in your brain and build positive forward momentum.

Kolbe and other personal assessment tools assist in laying new celebratory ski tracks by helping you accept the person you were naturally born to be and honor your unique traits. Instead of berating yourself for all that you aren't, begin to recognize all that you are.

For example, I am a big-picture person and my husband is brilliant with details. I have been hard on myself over the years for all of the invitations I've sent with typos and for my "deficiencies" regarding the practical aspects of family life, like keeping up with the calendar and managing all the moving parts in our lives. Now I simply own the fact that I always need detailed proofreaders and implementers in my life, and I rely on them heavily. In fact, if you find typos in this book, please take it up with my "detail team"—Scott, Peta, and Carolyn (all Ru-benstein's). Hopefully, we are all on the same page about the tiny details not being my strength and it won't ruin your impression of me. I may fail you grammatically, but I promise to deliver conceptually.

On average, 80 percent of our thoughts are negative or fear-based. Kinda scary, right? I have witnessed and experienced the magical opportunities that show up when the fear and guilt associated with negative thinking get booted out of the driver's seat. Learning to accept and celebrate yourself as the person you were born to be can be a super-effective antidote for self-sabotaging thoughts.

The daily report card exercise is a great tool to use as a beginning, realistic practice of sitting alone and daring to have positive thoughts about yourself and who you are as a person. My hope for you is that this quickly becomes not just a daily practice, but something you include in your life regularly. Celebratory thoughts about even the tiniest of accomplishments are like little self-confidence building blocks. Before you know it, your negative thinking about yourself will lessen and you will feel, look, and behave differently. You will invite more joy into your life. You know those people who seem to glow and radiate happiness? That will be you. And who doesn't want more joy?

Daily Report Card Exercise

Each night, as your head hits the pillow, find at least one example of something you did that day to celebrate about yourself. It could be as simple as, *I chose to sit and talk for five minutes with my child while he took a bath, rather than using the time to look at my phone.*

Decide to give yourself an A+ on something. Resist the urge at this moment to think of all that you need to improve on. I promise there are things you did really well in your day, and now is the time to list them and celebrate them—and you—as you send yourself off to sleep with loving, positive thoughts about yourself. Sweet dreams, Mama!

* * *

During the next step, if you have a secret quest for perfection, hang on tight, sister, because you may accidentally be your own worst enemy. Don't worry, we will begin to turn it around in just a few short pages.

CHAPTER 7

LETTING GO OF PERFECTION TO EMBRACE CONNECTION (CONCEPT 7)

"...If we live perfect, look perfect, and act perfect, we can minimize or avoid the pain of blame, judgment, and shame."

BRENÉ BROWN

SO THIS HAPPENED...

I want to tell you about Jill. Jill secretly worries that she is a bad mom. A typical nighttime scene in her home involves herself and her husband, David, lying in bed with headphones on, attached to their individual iPads, while their two kids flank the bed on either side desperately trying to get their parents' attention by whining, yelling, fighting, and basically pulling out all the stops. Somehow, amidst the chaos, Jill and David are able to ignore them and continue staring at their screens... invariably ending with David shouting at one of the kids and Jill shouting at David in defense of their child. The last thing Jill plans to do is silently sit back while David takes out his bad mood from his bad day and dead end job on their kids like her mom did when she was growing up. No ma'am. Not on her Mama-bear watch.

Do you relate to Jill? Do you relate to David? Do you feel like the clock's a-tickin' and you need to figure out how to create a happier family dynamic? STAT! Not to add to your hysteria, but, as we all know, the thing about kids is that they grow up and eventually become people who move out and live on their own without us. With that being said, time is of the essence to figure this out.

Jill considers herself to be extremely self-aware. She has a graduate degree in counseling and has read some parenting books as well as taken a ten-week conscious parenting course. She is angry with her herself and believes deep down that her laziness as a mom is the real reason that David loses his temper with the kids. If only she was the kind of mom that actually enjoyed being a mom and had the energy to interact with them in fun and playful ways like she always promised she would. Instead she finds herself feeling constantly exhausted and choosing her screen over engaging with her kids, as she believes a truly conscious parent would, and this belief adds to her cycle of guilt and shame.

What Jill doesn't understand yet is that being a conscious, engaged parent and fulfilling her dreams for a connected family can't be determined in a one-size-fits-all way. Every solution is different, even though the concepts are the same. We are each unique and different. It's most helpful—for Jill and for you and me—to stop measuring success based on another family's model. Imagine a perfection-connection continuum. Striving to be perfect in comparison with others involves being in a constant state of comparison and the need to conceal your *imperfections*. But your imperfections are what make you interesting and, most importantly, you. Because of this, a connected family will look different for everyone.

Jill had shown up consciously as a parent when she was in information-seeking mode and learning new parenting tools. However, when it came time to actually implement the new strategies, she found herself unable to recall the relevant tools amid the chaos and temper tantrums of the moment. She got lost deep in *The Parent Gap*. Within the gap, Jill chooses to numb out and distract herself with her screen rather than figuring out the source of her kid's neediness. No wonder Jill is constantly exhausted. The family culture is based on the kid's getting their attention seeking love cup filled by acting incredibly annoying and needy. I don't know about you but needy and annoying people are not enjoyable and I would probably check out too if I was Jill.

She often compares herself to the *neighbor's* model of what a happy, connected family looked like, and when her own reality looks different, Jill begins to judge herself and feels like a failure. Jill isn't enjoying motherhood or her children and based on the family dynamic, it is hard to imagine anyone that would enjoy walking a day in Jill's shoes.

In Jill's mind, the goal is to handle every situation with perfect patience and calmness, and her behavior as a mom must constantly reflect that unrealistic picture. When life actually happens, as it does, and she begins deviating from that "perfect" parent she has envisioned herself to be, she declares herself guilty with a sentence of life imprisonment, doomed to the black dungeon of "bad-mom-dom" while binge-eating or watching her screen mindlessly.

As long as Jill believes that narrative, she will continue to imprison herself in the guilt and isolation, in a land far away emotionally from her precious children and the connected family she has fantasized about since she was a child. One reverberating phrase plays on a continuous loop in her mind: "I think I'm screwing up my kids and failing miserably as a mom."

Jill believes there is no doubt that her kids will need to be in years of extensive therapy to get over all that she is doing wrong. She struggles with guilt and shame on a regular basis and often makes self-deprecating jokes about herself as a mom who is doing everything wrong. And even though she throws one hell of a kiddie birthday party down to the monogrammed party favors, and frequently posts pictures on social media suggesting an extremely happy and tight knit family unit, she confuses herself and others with her down to earth humor at her own expense. She attempts to convince herself and others that she accepts and celebrates herself and her faults fully and can even laugh at her imperfections. But in actuality, she spends a great deal of time distracting herself from her painful thoughts by binge eating, working, and constantly checking social media, to avoid thinking about her failure to be the perfect mom and to avoid how crappy she feels about herself.

I would like to set up a new possibility for Jill—and hopefully for you, too, if you see yourself anywhere in Jill's story. Imagine if Jill could see her life and her role as a conscious parent on that perfection-connection continuum. But with the understanding that the goal is never, ever to aim for perfect. The perfection side of the continuum is the opposite of where Jill truly wants to be. Her heart has always wanted connection and she was simply confused by her false belief that becoming the type of family that the neighbors envied would free her from negative judgment and hurt. On the connection side of the continuum, Jill understands that conscious parenting concepts, strategies, and examples all have the goal of helping her retrain the childhood destructive programming within her brain so that she can change her behavior and thoughts and *actually* build connected relationships. This is truly all she has ever wanted throughout her life. This is about realistic application. Striving for perfection is the enemy.

So how would the realistic application of the concepts in this book look for Jill? Well, for one thing, she would notice her thoughts enough to adjust her story about her parenting and change her story to realizing that she is a good person and a mom who loves her kids more than anything she has ever experienced. She would realize that unconditional love is her greatest gift to her kids. To be loved that intensely is powerful for children and, frankly, for anyone to experience. She would start leading with her heart more often, instead of beating herself up for not measuring up to the neighbors and to other people's *filtered* social media personas. She would allow her loving mama self to *enjoy* and to just love her kids, even if that looked like holding hands while watching television and eating junk food in bed.

Secondly, she would allow herself to feel tired at the end of a busy day and wouldn't equate being a tired mom with being a lazy mom. This would help her not leap from being tired to being exhausted by the guilt.

Thirdly, she would drop the "perfect mom" vision in her mind that looks like the parent who has endless energy for tickling, hugs, laughter, dance parties, playing board games, building forts, and playing blanket monster (blanket monster is a ridiculously dangerous game that my husband and kids used to play that resembled a WWF match and inevitably ended in tears—fun in theory, but in reality, one wrestling move away from the emergency room).

Fourth, in the evenings, Jill could say to her kids something like, "Crawl in here, you little monkeys, and watch a show with us—or play a game on my extra iPad while we snuggle and relax." Jill's family has multiple iPads and screens and phones—and that's okay (though the latest research speaks of the dangers of technology on child development... blah, blah, blah). Maybe Jill offers one of her earbuds to her daughter while her husband does the same with her son, and they listen to music or a funny story together. Or maybe they watch something borderline inappropriate on TV, something with too much violence and a few bad words, and Jill has to keep covering her kids' eyes or ears and fast-forwarding through the heavy-petting scenes.

I do believe that electronics and technology have to be managed and that too much of anything creates imbalance and distance in a family. I aim to spend more time away from technology when with my kids than with it.

However, some days, the bonding comes in the form of us hunkered down in my bed watching *old sitcoms on Netflix*. My point is, I love taking walks and talking or playing a game, but I also love watching television and laughing together with my kids. Realistically, every family I know uses technology as part of the equation. And that's okay in my book—everything in moderation in this modern world we live in.

I have come to learn that many moms have a fantasy in their minds of what their perfect family looks like. The images are a bit different for everyone. Some people envision one boy and one girl, with the boy being the protective big brother. Some may want all boys or all girls. Maybe you were an only child and your dream looks like the show *Eight is Enough* and you even plan to name your youngest son Nicholas (he was pretty adorable, after all).

Even though these fantasies seem harmless, they will keep you away from the connection part of the continuum— saway from your heart and from the inner knowing you have that can lead the way to a life in reality that's more connected. Visions of perfection have affected what many people post on social media, because they're trying to convince themselves and everyone else that they are living the fantasy—through the images they post. Here's the thing: if your fantasy is truly about having a connected and loving family, all of the pictures in the world and all of the "Likes" and approval from people who don't know what's true in your home can't create that reality. But you can.

The compare-and-despair hamster wheel phenomenon leaves a lot of folks feeling kind of crappy. That hamster wheel often leads to looking for and finding more ways to distract from the pain of reality. Scrolling through social media and wondering, deep down, why everyone else seems to have accomplished perfection, isn't going to get you where you want to be.

CONSCIOUS PARENTING LESSON AND SKILL: THE PERFECTION-CONNECTION CONTINUUM

Even though you would never admit it to anyone else, do you secretly want the perfect, connected fantasy family? Perfection is the enemy of connection. Read or listen to Brené Brown's work and you will find gobs of research about the negative side effects attached to perfectionism. Her TED Talk, a short twenty-minute talk, is a great introduction to her work (https://www.ted.com/talks/brene_brown_on_vulnerability?language=en). I am a parent who reads and studies concepts that are deeply examined by researchers like Brené. Like you, I pick and choose which concepts make sense to me and fit into my life. Then, in an effort to share that chocolate cake, I usually shout about the ones that have benefited me the most. The perfection-connection continuum falls into this category. It's so helpful I want to scream it from the rooftops to make sure you know about it.

Creating your version of your fantasy family, in reality, is an impossibility as long as you secretly remain on the hamster wheel of comparing your insides to others' outsides—the reason many of us feel like crap after scrolling through social media. Perfection is an illusion. I will go so far as to say that striving for perfection and behaving "perfectly," in a Facebook-post-worthy way, feels, to your body, like a claustrophobic straitjacket.

If I ignore that straitjacket feeling, I tend to be hard on my kids and unable to show up as the imperfect, but authentic and conscious, mama I am. Ignoring the straitjacket feeling can lead to saying ridiculous things to your kids like, "So-and-so won the spelling bee? Why don't you ever study for the spelling bee? If you aren't willing to go the extra mile, you won't get into a good college. Do you want to be mediocre in life?"

Do comments like those build more connection with your kiddos? Think about it. How does it feel when your parents or in-laws compare you to your sister-in-law, even in subtle ways? It may simply be that they are stating something awesome and definitely celebration-worthy about her, but you—through your body's whispers—can detect a tone of voice or manner that leaves you feeling less-than. Do you feel more *connected* to them in those moments?

Inadvertently, in an effort to set our kids up for success through achievement, we may push them to earn brag-worthy, resume-building awards by "encouraging" them through comparison types of comments—and leaving our kids feeling less-than.

The buried thought resulting in our harmful words usually has to do with the idea that being the best will protect our kids from negative judgment while earning them the respect and admiration of others. But your kids end up feeling pressured in a way that sabotages their connection with you, and—most likely—this will result in a combative, surly, or "shut-down" teenager.

CONSCIOUS PARENTING TOOL: STRAITJACKET OR SKINNY-DIPPING?

As I have learned to really pay attention to my body's whispers when I am triggered by situ-ations that cause old perfectionistic desires to surface, I am empowered to gracefully remove those identifiable triggers from my life altogether. For example, I avoid certain social situations that give me a feeling resembling dread. I have learned to decline invitations to functions where I know I will be surrounded by small-talking people with whom I don't feel safe to share my real self. Or, if accepting an invitation seems unavoidable, I make sure to saddle up with one or two people with whom I have a real connection. Quite often, that person is my husband.

Another example where I protect myself from unnecessary triggers is by managing my involvement in virtual communities like Facebook. I enjoy many aspects of social media, but I also have learned to set boundaries in terms of how I interact. I am not the most tech-savvy person, but I do know how to quietly unfollow Facebook friends whose posts trigger negative or competitive sensations within me. I choose to control my virtual involvement by simply not reading certain posts that feel braggy in nature rather than celebratory. The people who posted them may or may not actually be bragging, but the point is that it doesn't really matter whether they are or not. I choose to listen to my body's whispers and remove the triggers from my view without notifying the person who posted that I'm doing so. This is me taking my power back by avoiding an unnecessary trigger.

On a conscious level, I know that perfection is the enemy of connection. I also know that when I am in a triggered state, accessing the smartest part of my brain—my conscious mind—is unlikely. Therefore, I choose to eliminate situations that are easily avoidable when the strait-jacket feeling emerges. This makes space for more skinny dipping (relax, ladies, I am metaphorically referring to body whispers that feel like freedom).

For me, the skinny-dipping feeling of freedom occurs when I connect with like-minded people who increase, rather than deplete, my zest for life. Providing your-self with skinny-dipping opportunities (as a parenting tool, but if you like the stripped-down-naked version of the term, go for it!) creates positive momentum and deepens your connections with the people you love the most (especially the ones who get to experience the literal stripped-down you).

Straitjacket or Skinny-Dipping? Exercise

When you're making decisions in your life, it helps to envision the situation and consider the sensations you feel as you imagine having made the decision. Does imagining the experience leave you feeling calm but energized—like the feeling of skinny dipping, of gliding through the water without any self-consciousness? Or does it feel depleting, more like wearing a claustropho-bic straitjacket?

Think about a couple you sometimes double-date with and imagine being out to dinner with them. How do you feel in your body as you imagine being in that moment? Do you feel energized?

Notice the sensations in your body as you sit at the dinner table in the restaurant. Notice whether the imagined activity brings sensations to your body that represent skinny-dipping freedom (leading you toward connection), or straitjacket-claustrophobia (warning! perfectionism is lurking close by). Perfectionism creeps onto the scene when you feel a sense of comparison or less-than, and it results in the straitjacket feeling. Does imagining being out to dinner with this couple elicit feelings of competitiveness as they talk about their fabulous, superstar children or hang all over each other as they describe their active sex life, when you are experiencing a dry spell? Or... do you imagine the hours flying by, filled with stories that make you laugh until you pee and culminating in a discussion with your partner on the car ride home about how much you enjoy spending time with them?

This tool supports you by helping you create boundaries that allow you to reserve your energy for the people and situations in your life that matter the most to you. This will directly impact your connections with your people in such a good way.

This activity involves noticing and becoming aware of the messages your wise and protective body is whispering. You can decide to listen, or you can choose to ignore them until they scream... usually in the form of sleepless-ness and chronic pain or disease. Because, trust me, the body will only be ignored for so long. The straitjacket feeling will become increasingly more restrictive and claustrophobic if you continue to invite situations into your life that are not aligned with your truth.

The skinny-dipping feeling represents one of calmness, peace, and freedom from anything that feels constricting. It feels centered and unencumbered. Your body experi-ences a peaceful, natural, essential state, like the way you entered the world—dressed in nothing but your birth-day suit. The skinny-dipping feeling is devoid of tightness or tension in your body.

Your body knows that perfection is impossible. Striving for perfect is about resisting vulnerability by keeping yourself safe from negative judgment. Wouldn't you be safe from getting your feelings hurt if you were so perfect that there was nothing to criticize? Perfection isolates you and instigates feelings of loneliness, because you will keep others at arm's length in an effort to conceal your imper-fections and keep yourself in the safe-from-hurt zone.

Your body wants you to surround yourself with true com-munity, fulfilling your human need for love and belong-ing. This is why it sends you signals through its whispers. Brené Brown's amazing research and work about vulner-ability has taught me that it takes courage to share the real, authentic, imperfect, flawed version of myself with others. But this is how we build true connection. On the flip side, perfectionism strands you on an island all alone without a lifeboat.

* * *

Now that you understand how necessary it is to drop your desire for perfection, you are ready to tackle the biggie: *guilt*. At least, it is the biggie for Jews and Catholics. Can I say that, as a Jewish person? I hope I don't offend my Catholic friends. I'm not worried about the Jews—guilt is so rooted in our culture that I'm pretty sure it's covered in the Talmud.

I saved guilt for last because I think it is one of the most misunderstood and difficult emotions we encounter as parents. My experience and study of guilt has led me to believe that it is a dangerous emotion that promotes self-sabotage and the squashing of connected family dreams.

Don't worry, I've got your back. I will show you how to finally free yourself from the evil guilt saboteur so that nothing stands in your way of having the life and family you have always deeply craved.

CHAPTER 8

OY, THE GUILT

*"Guilt is anger directed at ourselves—
at what we did or did not do."*

PETER MCWILLIAMS

SO THIS HAPPENED...

Sara and Bill have been married for 13 years and have two beautiful children, a daughter who looks like Sara and a son who looks like Bill. They are an adorable family. About five years ago, I was their conscious parenting educator and coach. I have taught many other parents the same curriculum I used with Sara and Bill, and I credit these foundational concepts with shaping my little Rubenstein clan into a connected family.

Initially, Sara and Bill sought my help because their two young children were extremely high-energy, and their six-year-old daughter had received an autism spectrum disorder (ASD) diagnosis. Understandably, the couple was exhausted, and Sara suffered from intense guilt every time she handled a frustrating outburst from her daughter by dishing back matching frustration. Sara felt responsible for her daughter's unruly behavior, because she often found herself "losing it" alongside her child.

Before receiving the diagnosis, life felt hard all the time for the young family. Sara and Bill were constantly stressed out by their daughter's out-of-control tantrums, anger, and inability to interact kindly with her younger brother. They often intervened on their son's behalf, which usually concluded with yelling, insults, and behaving in ways toward their daughter that felt cruel and possibly even verbally abusive. The guilt Sara felt because of her reactions was enormous. She often thought to herself, *what type of mother yells, shames, and doesn't truly like her own child?* Sara found herself perpetually within *The Parent Gap,* wishing she was handling heated moments in a calm, controlled manner rather than acting like a lunatic alongside her struggling child. Deep down, Sara knew this destructive cycle would continue until she took control as the adult in the scenario and figured out a way to disrupt their current pattern. She secretly worried that she was doing irreparable damage to her daughter, whom she loved deeply and something had to change.

She also knew the tension and negative environment was affecting her young son as well.

Sara and Bill decided they had to do something. They had their daughter tested by a child psychologist and received the ASD diagnosis. When I met them, they were in resource-gathering mode regarding the autism assessment. They enrolled their daughter in a specialized school for ASD kids, and brought in a team of therapists and a parenting coach. Their willingness to handle challenges, face reality, and tackle their issues impressed me.

By the time Sara and Bill stopped working with me, they were well on their way to creating the connected family they both had always wanted growing up. Both Sara and Bill came from disconnected families but were determined to raise their kids differently. Interestingly, their daughter's diagnosis induced a sense of relief, as the stress they had been experiencing could be connected to a source and managed. They finally had an explanation for their frustration and misery and that relieved some of their guilt. Sara, especially, still struggled with the guilt to a certain extent, due to her angry behavior toward her daughter over the years in an effort to protect her son. She worried about the long-term damage she may have inflicted on her daughter. However, she tried her best to surround herself with resourceful support and move forward rather than looking back.

Having an ASD child can be extremely challenging to even the most patient of parents. I have noticed that the same-gendered parent as the ASD child seem to typically be more triggered by the ASD challenges. Sara was a case study. Her precious daughter looks like her physically and in many ways, Sara was living her childhood again vicariously through her daughter without realizing it. Her daughter's social challenges affected Sara more than she cared to admit, and her daughter's quirky and isolating behavior often left the sweet mama without being able to think clearly. After working with me prior, Sara knew the importance of controlling her own angry outbursts. By providing an emotionally safe environment in their home, her daughter was able to develop and thrive by living out of "defense mode," a crucial component in the ASD equation.

Time passed. As far as I knew, and according to Sara's Facebook posts, which I periodically "Liked", everything had been smooth sailing since I'd worked with Sara and Bill. However, when I met up with Sara about six months ago, I found out that Facebook wasn't the most reliable resource regarding their current state.

Sara had gained about 40 pounds and had started smoking again. Even though Sara doesn't yell and lose her temper like she did five years ago, she had fallen into some destructive patterns over the last year. She believed she knew what to do to be a "good" mom and was choosing not to do those things most of the time. As her daughter grew older, Sara found herself checking out more and more as a way to disengage and keep her cool when she felt like yelling at her "socially awkward" daughter. She felt intensely guilty, because she knew she *should* embrace her child's quirks—but she often found herself feeling worked up and even ashamed by her daughter's odd behavior. Therefore, Sara checks out in any way possible to try and distract herself and avoid those feelings that leave her feeling like a bad mom.

Sara is human and, right now, her distractions are taking priority—not as a choice, but as a necessity to help her deal with the triggered emotions from her own unfinished business as a girl.

Most moms are affected by their daughters' social standing and lives. This is an uncomfortable thing to admit to yourself, let alone to anyone else. I can speak to this personally. As my daughter entered sixth grade, I was shocked to find out how much the middle school issues affected me! I was a parent coach, after all, and had been teaching conscious parenting classes for years. Luckily, my triggered reactions were caught quickly, with the help of my conscious daughter, who wanted to know what the hell had happened to her typically level-headed mama. One day, as my mouth began doling out some really lame advice after an incident she'd had with the "queen bee" at her school, my daughter said to me, "Mom, are you telling me to respond to her with snarky sarcasm?" When she asked me that so candidly, I realized that I was operating on autopilot from an old ski track and wasn't speaking from my conscious brain. By the next day, we were able to have a productive convo about triggers, *"girl world"* drama, and the brain. I love that story, because my daughter and I have referred back to it over and over again. It was a great example of a mistake on my part providing a valuable learning opportunity.

After experiencing the triggers of my own unfinished business as a result of my developing daughter's social encounters, I can only imagine how Sara and other moms of ASD children feel. It makes perfect sense to me why Sara was relying on her old, distracting behaviors in an attempt to feel better. It helped her to avoid losing her temper—possibly shaming her daughter for Sara's own unresolved issues. Unfortunately, Sara's guilt prevented her from seeing the situation clearly enough to offer compassion to herself and ask for support.

Sara believes she is consciously choosing all of the ways she distracts herself—food, tech-nology, binge-watching TV, cigarettes, work, drinking at night with girlfriends, and online shopping—instead of engaging with her kids. She feels enormous guilt about this and, underneath the guilt, she feels shame for continuing this cycle that feels eerily similar to the distanced style of her parents when she was a child. Essentially, Sara feels guilt on top of shame. And yet she still continues on the path of repeating the unhealthy patterns.

According to the Merriam-Webster dictionary, the definition of *guilt* is: *feelings of culpability especially for imagined offenses or from a sense of inadequacy*. Notice the terms *imagined offenses* and *sense of inadequacy*. Guilt is a villainous monster that inhibits growth because it creates *imagined* stories in your mind based on your feelings of all that you are not. F*#k that noise! How on earth are we going to show up as the kickass leaders of our families with that kind of self-sabotage going on?

Sara is a perfect example of guilt sabotaging her family connections. She believes that her inadequacy as a mom due to *imagined offenses* is quite real, considering the proof provided by her distracting behaviors. She feels guilty and ashamed because she believes she consciously chooses to distract herself rather than accepting her daughter as the amazing child she was born to be.

Sara desperately *wants* to raise her kids differently. Unfortunately, her shame-distraction-guilt cycle intensifies the pain left over from her unhealed childhood wounds, so she doesn't seem to stand a chance of changing the unhealthy patterns. The shame is rooted in all the ways she felt dismissed, unloved, and unhappy as a kid. She feels intensely shameful and guilty every time she believes, deep down, that she is behaving the way her mom did by using some form of distraction as an attempt to feel better—even though she has learned better ways and has a higher level of awareness than her mom had. This is the shame cycle, and it has a powerful hold on sweet Sara, who believes she is a conscious parent poser.

Sara feels intensely lonely, like she is existing on an island by herself. The lack of feeling love and belonging, due to the shame and guilt she feels daily, has resulted in isolating herself from those she loves, as well as from authentic friendships. She feels she has no real community. This phenomenon has left a gaping hole that she attempts to fill with even more distracting behaviors. All she really wants is to feel better.

Unfortunately, as long as guilt is on the scene, Sara's situation will not improve. Guilt sabotages healing and growth. When guilt appears, shame is close by. Guilt reinforces all of Sara's *imagined offenses* by shining a spotlight on the reasons for her perceived inadequacy, selfishness, and not being enough.

Sara now regrets not reaching out to me sooner. The guilt she felt for not accepting and embracing her daughter as the ASD kid she was born to be was the main culprit for her avoidance of dealing with how bad her life had gotten. As a parent who had learned conscious parenting tools, Sara felt ashamed and embarrassed to deny her daughter's eccentricities, and that prevented her from contacting me.

This is a perfect example of shame requiring secrecy to survive, and guilt providing just the right incubator to grow and preserve the shame. Sara is now learning to accept her humanity, work through her own old wounds that have resurfaced as her daughter grows older, and give herself love and compassion. She is learning to mother herself the way she would have loved to have been mothered when she was a child. This allows her to show up for her kids as the conscious, nurturing, accepting, and loving mother she has always been in her heart.

CONSCIOUS PARENTING LESSON AND SKILL: CONQUERING THE GUILT MONSTER

Isn't guilt a consequence I deserve to feel for making bad decisions? Doesn't it help me to hold myself accountable, so I can strive to be a better parent?

I have heard guilt described as the lesser of two evils compared to shame. I believe the two emotions love to slow dance together when it comes to parenting. When guilty feelings and thoughts enter your home, shame is lurking close by.

Guilt can be an effective motivator in the short term, but it will ultimately leave you feeling worse and will lead to more behaviors that you will feel guilty and ashamed about later. I have heard guilt described as a selfish emotion. Think about it—when you're feeling guilty, even though it may look like you are thinking about your actions and how they affect others, are you completely self-consumed with all the examples and reasons you believe you're inadequate? Does anyone else truly enter your mind? Or is your thinking completely self-focused as you beat yourself up for all that you have done wrong? Are you really thinking about your kids during guilty moments? Or do you stay stuck, lost in negative judgmental thoughts all about yourself?

Giving in to the guilt monster is absolutely not productive in closing *The Parent Gap*. What helps is having access to tools and strategies that build connection within your family. Using them to create a more compassionate story that's based on the foundational concepts presented in this book is a great way to close the gap and show up as the parent you truly are in your heart.

Although Sara desired deep connection, it remained absent in her life until she started addressing her own unhealed wounds. She was repeating the cycle with her children by relying on distractions to feel better, instead of bonding, connecting, and accepting her children, which is the true antidote. She can break the family patterns passed down to her by practicing connecting strategies, instead of remaining on autopilot and using distractions to escape the lonely and painful feelings she had been experiencing daily.

Guilt would continue to isolate Sara, causing her to turn to distracting behaviors. Guilt, as a selfish emotion, propelled her to partake in activities to feel better that ultimately caused her to feel more alone. Learning to invite compassion into her life rather than guilt, Sara can begin choosing purposefully to connect with her family during triggered moments instead of turning to shame and repeating the pattern of disconnection. Using the tools presented in the previous chapters, Sara can retrain her brain and body to feel better.

Change begins with awareness. As Sara uncovers her distraction patterns to understand when and why they occur, she will build self-awareness. She will use her body as an insightful resource by tuning in to her body's whispers and seeing her guilt as a messenger meant to alert her to the shame stories underneath. By sitting with the sensations of her body and uncovering the painful thoughts behind her body's whispers, she can turn to the excavated stories from her past and continue to connect the dots of the unhealthy patterns from her childhood that she seeks to change. Understanding the roots of her story will help her to compassionately embrace her humanness and her human desire to feel better as a result of her longing for connection.

CONSCIOUS PARENTING TOOL: THE MATCHING GAME

I love the saying *what we focus on grows*. The brain seeks patterns. It looks for those well-worn-in ski tracks to go back to again and again. Guilt puts the focus on all that you are doing *wrong*. As you focus on all that is bad about you—your behavior, your life, remaining stuck in the blame—you will remain stuck in the old and not be able to lay new, healthier ski tracks.

To show up as a conscious parent, focus on all that you are doing well, while offering yourself compassion and the right to be imperfectly human. Replacing feelings of guilt with the space to make mistakes and the intention to forgive yourself allows you to brush yourself off and begin again, rather than remaining mired down in the shame-distract-guilt cycle. As Sara's story illustrates, no amount of conscious parent training will retrain your brain if you allow the guilt monster to take over. Even when that training is delivered by a *highly* supportive and effective coach.

Playing the Matching Game can help you break the shame-distract-guilt cycle.

The Matching Game Exercise

1. Notice and become aware of it when the guilt cycle is happening for you (shame-distract-guilt). The noticing will naturally occur as you learn to listen to your body's whispers and identify your triggered moments.

2. Identify the triggering circumstance that led to the coping behavior, inducing the feeling of being alone, splashing in a puddle of guilt. Can you also identify the root, old story, or limiting belief that's attached to the upsetting situation? What caused your upset? Can you think of another time in your life when you felt similar sensations?

3. Match every reason that supports a feeling of guilt with a compassionate reason. Understanding, with compassion, that you continue unhealthy behaviors in order to feel better, will support your healing and growth and ability to lean on a new, healthier coping mechanism.

Here's an example of the Matching Game in action:

1. *Notice the shame-distract-guilt cycle:* "I hid from the kids in my room, binging on candy and reality television rather than spending quality time with them after school."

2. ***Triggering circumstance:*** "My husband, John, called 30 minutes before the appointment with the child psychologist, to let me know he wouldn't be coming. He knows we need help with our daughter and he chose work, again, over prioritizing our family's needs. Our daughter, Ruthie, has shut down and has been skipping meals and refusing to interact with anyone in the family. She constantly wears baggy clothes to disguise her alarmingly shrinking body. I'm really worried that she may have an eating disorder and is in serious trouble. I swore that my kids would have a loving and present father, un-like what I experienced growing up. My dad was an absent father who seemed like he was more in love with his job than my mom—or his kids, for that matter."

3. ***Match a compassionate reason to a reason for guilt:*** *Reason for guilt:* "I chose to numb myself and pump toxins into my body, even though I claim to value being healthy. I'm a total hypocrite and, to make matters worse, I chose to be absent by checking out from my kids, rather than being a present and engaged mom. Am I really any different than my husband... or my father?" *Compassionate reason:* "I'm really worried about Ruthie. Eating disorders are very serious and

they're especially triggering for me because I struggled with bulimia during my teen years. Ruthie is only 13—far too young to be dealing with this type of problem. I never felt supported by my dad and I used food to fill the emptiness within me that was probably a result of his absence in my life. When John cancelled such an important meeting regarding our daughter being in crisis, I felt abandoned all over again. This hits so close to home, because I see the pattern repeating for Ruthie that I experienced. The pain felt too big and I resorted to my old methods to feel better. I have overcome so much myself, but this time I used my old distractions—sugar and television—to cope with being upset. I will do everything possible to support and connect with Ruthie, even if that means I have to show up as both Mom and Dad. Next time, I will choose to connect with Ruthie rather than matching her experience by isolating myself."

* * *

Addressing guilt is the final step in closing *The Parent Gap* to stay calm, cool, connected and to be able change destructive patterns. Guilt often serves as your autopilot programming, reinforcing the old ski tracks in your brain and convincing you that you don't deserve the connected family you fantasized about years before. To combat the guilt monster and keep it from sabotaging your healing and growth, practice the tools in this book. They'll help you use self-compassion as a way to create healthier patterns in your family and life. You have used the distractions to lessen your guilty body whispers triggered by reminders of old, unhealed wounds. Now you are learning powerful tools and a new path of coping that will result in filling the emptiness inside with deep, rich, meaningful connections.

You CAN retrain your brain and be the parent you always wanted to be even during the hard moments with your kids. Becoming a conscious parent and living by the concepts discussed within these pages will support you in closing *The Parent Gap* so that you can build your connected family dream team once and for all! By focusing on strengthening family connections and reenvisioning your old fantasy to include your perfectly imperfect family, new and healthier patterns and habits will emerge. With compassion and self-acceptance taking the place of guilt, shame, and distraction, you've got this, Mama!

CHAPTER 9

LET'S DO THIS, LADIES!

*"The world will be saved by the
Western woman."*

THE DALAI LAMA AT THE
VANCOUVER PEACE SUMMIT, 2009

By now you have a decent framework for understanding the reality of your situation, and that it's downright counterproductive to sit all alone in the dark with painful underlying thoughts: *The clock is tickin' away and none of us seem to be having a heck of a lot of fun here. What if their memories when they think back on their childhood are filled with images of me screaming my head off at them or saying rude things. What if they have no stand out happy memories because I was too tired to be playful and we spent our days immersed on our individual technology "nocializing" for hours and never spending quality time as a family?*

What if they grow up and want to live far, far away from me tomorrow because of all I'm doing today?

If these worries continue to plague you, your limiting beliefs have a strong hold. You have options when it comes to retraining your brain and freeing yourself from the beliefs that limit you and prevent you from being the parent you want to be. You can continue to reread this book, do further research, and work the tools and concepts. That has mostly been my path toward healing. This is the reason I wrote this book and created a program to complement it. I would love to have had that option when I was where you are right now.

Coaching programs produce results faster than you can typically accomplish on your own. The issue of accountability also makes your success far more likely when working with a coach in your corner. If you are interested in talking with me about your specific situation, and to find out if the program is right for you, visit me at http://www.randirubenstein.com/.

If you're still saying to yourself, *Yeah, but you don't know me well enough to fully get how bad a parent I really am. I mean, my secret behavior and neglect are off the rails. I am far too embarrassed to talk about it with you, or with anyone!* Or maybe you're thinking that you can't possibly pull off this healing process because it involves releasing resentment about the past and there are really good reasons why you have chosen not to *excavate your stories* and release the anger and resentment. Those scars run deep and far exceed something as minor as 1970s hands-off parents. I gotta say, I completely hear you and I do actually *get* it. I have had deeply embedded scars, too. When I tell you that old wounds can be like an under the skin pimple to heal—you know the ones, the painful cystic type that can feel like a small planet taking root right on your face for the world to see. My journey has been long and arduous—to the tune of 18 years—I am not exaggerating. I get it.

If you're still feeling like the concepts in this book can't help you, you may be right. If you aren't willing to do the work because *misery feels like home* and you're cozy at home, that's cool. From my viewpoint, if you are still reading, we have shared a decadent piece of rich chocolate cake, and now you're telling me that you'd thought you might be a chocoholic, but—even though the cake *was* absolutely delicious—you've decided to embrace Key lime pie from now on. Really? Unless you have a chocolate allergy, Key lime over chocolate cake is hard to wrap my head around. And, just so you know, if your scars seem way too deep and overwhelming to begin this process on your own... that's why I created my coaching programs. I am literally a website away, at http://www.randirubenstein.com/.

If you find yourself with a voice in your head right now that sounds a lot like Debbie Downer, be aware that your old ski tracks are well-worn-in, and creating new, fresh tracks will take lots of repetition and the help of someone trained in these techniques. Your brain was programmed a long time ago, so it might take a minute or more to override those old scripts and create new neural pathways. And, by the way, I wasn't calling you old. You look great. Really.

This book reflects my own journey and much of what I have learned while raising my kids and getting the connected family I fantasized about as a little fifth-grade girl so long ago—and, yes, I'm calling myself kind of old. I have done the heavy lifting for you: researching, reading, teaching, and constantly experimenting in my test kitchen with my three little pigs at home. *(Guinea pigs,* people. My kids are my guinea pigs. It's a joke.)

Provided within these pages is a *realistic* foundation for you to immediately begin this process of healing, growth, evolution, connection, and, ultimately, divine happiness. *And,* please remember that your #1 assignment is to embrace who you were born to be, drop the perfect image or expectation you may have placed on yourself, and engage authentically with your kids. The bottom line is that your kids really want to know *you.* Getting to know, understand, and cheer for yourself will allow you to bring your whole self into the relationship and this will be the nucleus of your connected family. Sharing the authentically awesome *you* with your people is a generous gift and will eliminate those guilty thoughts surrounding your failure to be the *perfect* mother. Striving for that ridiculous image of perfection causes the real damage and prevents true connection.

As I see it, moms have the power to shape the next generation. We are the primary parent in the majority of households and, as Dr. Bruce Lipton taught us, our brains are programmed during childhood by the people with whom we spend the most time. That would be the mamas, in most cases. We have the opportunity to mold and shape our kids into the people that we want to see in charge in the future. But first we have to feel better so we can accomplish that goal. Let us step into our positive leadership role, together, as a community, and begin changing the world—one connected family at a time.

The concepts laid out in this book will provide a solid basis for you to close *The Parent Gap* and begin to focus on creating more of what you want rather than spending your time feeling guilty for all the things that you think define your inadequacies.

THANK YOU

If you would like to check out what my connected clan looks like, I've created something special for you. I can't wait to hear what you think, because I don't want our time together to end!

Go to *http://www.randirubenstein.com/* to sign up and check out my 5 part reality series, True Confessions of a Connected Family.

Tune in as I turn the camera on myself and my family for your "reality-loving" viewing pleasure. Of course, there will be some great nuggets of connected family secrets mixed in with the jokes (which are mostly at my expense). As you know by now, I have read truckloads of parenting and self-help books. I am always curious about the author and what their family *really* looks like behind closed doors. In this four-part short video series, you will:

- See with your own eyes what I and my people look, sound, and act like (in case you've been curious).

- Find out from my kids' perspectives what my flaws are and how my flaws have impacted them.

- Hear what my kids love about our family.

- Take a walk down memory lane with us and learn about the best conscious parenting tools I used with them when they were younger (of course, I'm still using them all now, but they don't need to know that, right?).

- Witness *real*, organic conversations between me and my kids and see what being a connected family looks like for us.

- Be inspired and begin to imagine what *your* new, connected fantasy family looks like, and learn how I can help (if you are a quick-start, like me, and were ready yesterday!).

Go to *http://www.randirubenstein.com/* for access to the reality series.

ABOUT THE AUTHOR

Randi Rubenstein helps parents change unhealthy patterns—including ones that are passed down through the generations—to create loving and connected families. She is an author, parent coach and most importantly, a fellow mama in the trenches devoted to growing her people to be healthy and whole. Randi's specialty is helping parents close *The Parent Gap*— the gap between the calm loving parent you always intended to be and the parent you currently are during challenging moments with your kiddos. She believes it's time to replace the dominant parenting methods of yesteryear involving fear, threats and yelling, with a nurturing and assertive approach that leaves no room for guilt or worry that you are screwing up the most important role of your life—raising your kids.

She lives in Houston, Texas, with her husband of twenty years, their three kids, two dogs and two part-time cats.

You can find find out more about Randi and her programs at *http://www.randirubenstein.com/*.

Morgan James
Speakers Group

We connect Morgan James published authors with live and online events and audiences whom will benefit from their expertise.

Morgan James makes all of our titles available
through the Library for All Charity Organization.

www.LibraryForAll.org